It's Showtime!

Richard Butterfield's Power of Persuasion

Communication and Presentation Skills
for Every Profession

by Richard Butterfield

edited by Steven Young

San Francisco, California

2014

D1122666

Copyright 2014
Richard Butterfield
Published with the assistance of Stephanie Jackel and Printer's Ink
Cover design by Erik Casillas

All rights reserved. No part of this publication may be reproduced in any form or
by any means without the prior written permission of Richard Butterfield, 96 Mirabel
Avenue, San Francisco, CA 94110 www.butterfieldspeaks.com.

ISBN-13: 978-0-9853338-2-9 (for softcover book)
ISBN-13: 978-0-9853338-3-6 (for e-book)
Library of Congress Control Number: 2014908842

It's Showtime!

Richard Butterfield's Power of Persuasion

Communication and Presentation Skills for Every Profession

Dedication

For my father

As a boy growing up in Hingham, Massachusetts, I romanticized my father's life. He ran a CBS television station that was sorely in need of a turn-around man when he arrived. Hero that he was, he pushed the station's local newscast to #1 in the market. He had already done the same thing at a station in Minneapolis and he would go on to do it again in Portland, Oregon. But in Hingham, I actually imagined workers at the station cheering for him. In fact, I still have a 5th grade writing assignment in which I described all those passionate employees chanting "RJB! RJB! Who's the greatest? RJB!"

As I grew older, I looked back with some embarrassment on my youthful fantasies of my father's work life. Who in their right mind would cheer a business executive? But today, I coach people like my father. And I've learned that, while people may not actually stand up and cheer, they do something much more powerful – they engage, they join, they find purpose and bet their futures on persuasive leaders like my dad.

Here's to you, RJB – you were the greatest.

It's Showtime!

Richard Butterfield's Power of Persuasion

In 2008 I launched *It's Showtime! Butterfield Speaks on the Power of Persuasion*. Today thousands of professionals are accelerating their success using the strategies and skills from this popular book.

Using *Powerbites*, CEO's are delivering concise and persuasive messages to drive success. Change leaders are using *Aspirational Storytelling* to shape an inspiring vision. Sales teams are applying *Active Listening Skills* to better hear and understand the needs of their prospects. Keynote speakers are using the *Hook, Promise, and Roadmap* to differentiate their presentations. And spokespeople are using the *Q&A Playbook* to navigate tough question and answer scenarios.

This third edition, *It's Showtime! Richard Butterfield's Power of Persuasion*, reflects my commitment to sharpen and expand on the book. I have refreshed many of the chapters while adding insights culled from current client engagements. New topics and best practices have emerged from my work as a presentation skills coach, strategic message consultant, speech writer and media trainer. This third edition includes an expanded section on Media Savvy because – as we all know – every presentation is a potential media event. And, finally, I trust you will appreciate the vivid and readable format that makes for easier access to key concepts and takeaway ideas.

Richard Butterfield
San Francisco, CA
May 2014

Table of Contents

The Power of Persuasion

The Passion to Persuade

We've all seen them, heard them, experienced their power. In business, education, the arts and media and, of course, politics. They are the CEOs who emerge from the executive ranks. The gurus who guide the experts. The true teachers who stand out among the educators. The statesmen and women who rise above mere politicians and officeholders.

What they say, and how they say it, has the power of persuasion. With that power, they command not just attention but allegiance. They inspire. By giving voice to their vision, they convince us that we see it, too. Like Prometheus, they bring us a gift of fire, kindling their passion in our hearts and minds. Through the power of persuasion, they make things happen. They move and they shake. They change the world – or at least they change minds, which is the same thing.

How can we understand their peculiar genius? Are they "naturals" – prodigious talents sprung full-blown from the gene pool? Do they have more brainpower or willpower, exceptional competitive drive, or the ineffable quality we call charisma?

Maybe they're simply more glib than the rest of us, blessed with the gift of gab and nerves of steel. Maybe they're better at thinking and talking "on their feet," as the expression goes. Or maybe they're just plain lucky – fortunate enough to be linked by history to a welcome message, a winning product, a prosperous enterprise, or a great cause.

After all, few people in history have had or ever will have the oratorical power of Lincoln or Churchill or Martin Luther King Jr., much less an opportunity to use that power to save a nation or advance a cause. Only a handful are both forceful and fortunate enough to imprint their passion on public perception and drive revolutions in business and technology, as Jack Welch, Steve Jobs, and John Chambers have done.

But look closer to home. Most of us have known exceptional communicators in our own lives and careers – friends and colleagues, mentors and managers with a talent and zest for touching others through the spoken word.

Look near as well as far, and you'll find that the passion to persuade is alive and at work every day, in everyone's life, including yours.

Exceptional communicators change the world with the spoken word.

All the World's a Stage.

I devoted much of my education to becoming an actor, and I started my career as a theater person. I "pounded the boards" in college productions at Stanford. I earned my master's degree in acting at the American Conservatory Theater in San Francisco, and later became Dean of the Conservatory. Meanwhile, I enjoyed several years of success as an actor, director, and teacher of theater arts in the Bay Area (and yes, a little bit in Hollywood).

During those years it never occurred to me that the craft I was practicing might be valuable, or even useful, for more than performing Shakespeare and Sondheim.

But, like most people, I kept up with the careers of friends and acquaintances in business, law, medicine, engineering, and other fields. All of these people were smart and capable. Many were truly exceptional. Yet, while some excelled and advanced as I expected they would, others seemed slow to fulfill their potential. It started me wondering about the latter group: did they lack some ingredient, some gift or skill, for success?

Then one day a trio of lawyers walked into my office at the American Conservatory Theater and asked me a simple question: "Can you help lawyers succeed, in the courtroom and beyond, by teaching them the skills used in theater?" My answer was "Yes," and my journey had begun.

My transition from actor, teacher, and director to communications consultant was inspired by the realization that the arts of the theater could be enormously useful to virtually everyone with drive and determination, whatever their field or profession.

The intense pursuit of an objective. The importance of clarity and focus. The impact of brevity. The art of storytelling. The meaning and power of body language. The effective use of the voice. And the value of preparation, practice, and rehearsal.

> Lessons from acting can fuel your power of persuasion.

These are the elements that make up the power of persuasion. And they have just as much to do with presenting yourself effectively as they do with an actor's portrayal of Lady Macbeth, Willy Loman, Eliza Doolittle, or Cyrano de Bergerac. They come into play in a board meeting, a product launch, a press briefing, a client conference, a trial or negotiation, and hundreds of other presentations and interactions in business and professional life.

In short, these skills and techniques work as powerfully in the workaday world and everyday life as they do in the make-believe realm of the theater. They can and do help people succeed at work, in their careers, even in their personal lives. And they are available to all of us.

The Many Uses of Persuasion

Richard Butterfield's Power of Persuasion is a guide for people who want to learn, develop, and master the art of persuasive communication through the spoken word.

The approach described here, which I call the Power of Persuasion for short, has been developed and refined during hundreds of workshops, coaching sessions, media trainings, and rehearsals. It has helped people in business, technology, healthcare, law, advertising, and other professions. It will prepare you to succeed in press events, client conferences, roadshows, tradeshows, speeches, and business pitches.

Beyond preparing for specific events, you can count on the skills and techniques developed through the power of persuasion to help bring discipline and alignment to your company's branding, product positioning, and public relations. By crafting compelling messages and delivering them effectively in both normal and challenging circumstances – not only in one-to-many presentations and encounters, but also in one-on-one relationships – you'll be able to win agreement and change minds in your organization, your industry, the marketplace, and the forum of public opinion.

The power of persuasion is not about leadership as such, although I've coached many leaders and participated in many executive development programs. This is no accident. After all, communication is the action of leadership. It's the means that leaders use to translate their intellectual brilliance or political instincts or market insight or decision-making acumen into action. It's the way they project their will in the world, persuading others to believe, to join, to act. But those are challenges for all of us, not for leaders only. And so is the power of persuasion.

How This Book Is Organized

This book is divided into three major sections.

Part I: "Accessing the Power of Persuasion Within"

This section covers the personal preparation necessary before you can either craft an effective message or communicate it successfully –

- getting in touch with your professional passion and making sure you have the "victor, not victim" attitude

- developing the listening skills you need to know and connect with your audience to get across "what's in it for them"

- clarifying your vision so you can share it with others

Mastering the Power of Persuasion will help you win hearts and minds.

Part II: "Discovering and Developing Your Message"

This section is a guide to creating clear, compelling messages –

- preparation; assessing the risks and opportunities of the engagement, your objectives and the obstacles

- identifying the core of your message, or your "message mantra"

- "powerbites," storytelling, and other techniques for making your message memorable and portable

- structuring a winning presentation

Part III: "Mastering Your Craft as a Communicator"

This section provides tips and techniques for developing your tools as a speaker –

- the power of the voice

- taking control: acting as producer, director, and designer of your "show"

- stage presence; finding power positions, using expressive gestures and projecting confidence

- how to rehearse effectively and efficiently

- turning question and answer into question and message.

The Power of Persuasion is within your grasp!

Appendices provide tips for dealing with pre-presentation nerves and a guide for evaluating presentations, your own and others'.

At the end of certain chapters you'll find exercises for practicing and developing various communication skills. I urge you to use them on your own or with a colleague or friend to prepare, practice, and develop your power of persuasion.

Preparation, practice, development – these are three excellent notes on which to end this introduction, because mastering the power of persuasion is not a mystery. It's a matter of discovering and developing the passion to persuade, and the skills and techniques for doing so, that we all have within us.

Chapter 1

Three Truths About Attitude

Persuasion Starts with Attitude.

It may be true that many great speakers are born, not made. But consider the story of Demosthenes.

> As a youth in Athens, he had a speech impediment, and he was jeered the first time he addressed a large public assembly. He could have given up, but instead he unleashed his passion to persuade. To learn to speak distinctly, Demosthenes practiced talking with pebbles in his mouth and recited poetry while running. To strengthen his voice, he went to the seashore and declaimed over the roar of the waves. And to learn to craft compelling messages, he worked as a speech writer for many years. Demosthenes combined drive with rigorous practice to make himself into an orator – the greatest, we are told – in ancient Greece.

The story of Demosthenes reminds us that anyone can become a great presenter. It should also remind us that the *power* to persuade begins with the *passion* to persuade.

The power to persuade begins with the passion to persuade.

The Passion to Persuade

To be an exceptional persuader, you must define and give voice to your professional passion. You must share this professional passion. You must catch yourself communicating with passion. And most important, you must use this passion to fuel all of your persuasions.

In my years of coaching, I've observed that inspiring communicators instinctively know how to bring passion – a twinkle in the eye – to their communications.

> "I was on a bike ride. Had an idea." That's how Gary Erickson describes the epiphany that led to his founding Clif Bar, the natural foods maker that became one of the fastest-growing companies in America. But with Gary, you don't hear standard CEO-talk about innovation or first-mover advantage. You hear about good nutrition, about wholesome products, about sustaining employees and communities and the planet. You understand why Gary rejected a nine-figure buy-out and kept

control of his company. And you're glad he did, because you feel as if he did it for you.

*

Laura Alber, CEO of Williams Sonoma, radiates a sense of mission and purpose. Her passion for the customer is prevalent in all her leadership communications. For everyone on her team, the phrase, "I am at your service" is message and mantra. This singular focus helps Laura drive a culture of excellence across all her leading brands.

*

Jeff Weiner, well known for his leadership of LinkedIn and his successes at Yahoo, has a reputation inside and outside his company as an inspiring thought-leader. Ask him about social networks and consumers on the Web and you understand why. You're quickly swept up in Jeff's inspiring vision of all the "What if?" and "Why not?" possibilities for the future. You share his vision because you want to, and you can't wait to see it become a reality.

*

Dr. Robert Pearl is CEO of Northern California's Permanente Medical group, which includes thousands of Kaiser Permanente doctors. In all his communications, Dr. Pearl combines a surgeon's keen focus with an exuberant intellectual energy. When he talks to physicians about what they can do to improve patient care, he combines his encyclopedic knowledge with the sheer intensity of his belief to create an inspiring, contagious vision of a better, more effective way of practicing medicine.

Leaders like these have a connection with their mission that is visceral in the original sense of that word: they feel it in their gut. And when we listen to them, we feel it, too. Passion is contagious. When we sense it in a speaker, we share it; the speaker's mission becomes our mission. That's why tapping into what really moves you is so important to developing your power of persuasion.

Dig deep to identify why your work is important to you.

Call it your mission, your passion, your motivation – when connecting with it comes naturally to you, great! But when it doesn't … what then? Then you have to work at it. You have to work at identifying what's important to you. You have to define your mission. You have to uncover your passion.

Uncovering Your Professional Passion

I often begin my coaching engagements by asking clients to describe their professional passion. For many, this simple question unleashes a compelling narrative. They immediately become more animated and speak with enthusiasm and a sense of urgency.

For many, a description of professional passion is difficult. Instead, I ask these people to tell me the story of their most pride-filled moment as a professional. I ask for the "Once upon a time, and then one day, and I'll never forget the moment when" story. By coaching them into storytelling, I help them uncover and give voice to their professional passion.

Within their stories, we discover powerful attributes or values. Stories of brilliant calculation, team work or entrepreneurial spirit. Stories where there is a passion for transformation, problem solving or doing well by doing good. By asking yourself fundamental questions about your motivations, you unlock your professional passion. And when you bring this professional passion to life by describing it out loud, you'll catch yourself speaking and caring at the same time. This is the passion that must infuse all of your persuasions.

Catch yourself speaking and caring at the same time.

Your Statement of Professional Passion

Asking core questions and considering seminal stories is an important step on the road to honing your professional passion. Everyone should have an urgent professional mission or passion. Do not be afraid of embracing yours. Envision what you want to achieve, what you want to be, and what you want your professional world to be. Give voice to your statement of professional passion and test it with a friend, colleague, spouse, or partner. This content will serve you in myriad future situations: inspiring a team, recruiting a like-minded professional, profiling yourself and your work, or interviewing for a job.

Here is an example of my professional passion.

> As an actor, I often experienced those magical moments when great drama, well performed, moves an audience of hundreds of people to hold their breath in suspense, gasp with horror, or laugh with relief as if they were one person. I also loved to teach. For years, I had the privilege of sharing my knowledge in scene study, voice, and musical theatre classes with young artists who grew into their own talents before my eyes. When I brought those two parts of my training and experience together, and started teaching business and professional people how to master the art of communication, I found a new sense of purpose that energizes and enriches my life to this day. It is simply enormously satisfying to me – and incredibly fun – to help smart, committed people experience their own power of persuasion.

You may have to dig deep.

Here's an example of someone who had to do some digging to uncover her passion.

> This executive had been given responsibility for emergency preparedness across multiple facilities of a large regional healthcare provider – a big job, and one that would require her to win the cooperation and orchestrate the efforts of many people. In my early

training sessions with her, she came off as a dull, uninspired, and uninspiring speaker. She didn't communicate any sense of mission and it was hard to feel there was anything at stake.

So we did some exploring. How had she come into her new job? Why did she care about what she was doing? What drew her to this career? Talking about such things brought her around to some disaster relief work she'd done years ago. As she recalled the devastation and loss, the shock and grief of those who suffered, she became emotional. Through this courageous exploration, her mission came into focus. The stakes were very high indeed. By preparing people for emergencies, she wanted to avert the suffering that occurs when disaster strikes. Most important, she found a way to infuse this passion into her communications. Now she commands attention by starting her presentations with a powerful story from her own experience. She keeps her audiences engaged with a new-found zing in her voice and a sparkle in her eyes.

The lesson here is simple: People don't care how much you know until they know how much you care.

We don't care how much you know until we know how much you care.

When you discover and bring the appropriate level of passion to all your communications – from the one-on-one to the board room or keynote stage – you will have what it takes to be more persuasive.

Active Communication — It's Your Job, Bob.

Unless you're in marketing or public relations, you might not consider yourself responsible for an ongoing communications campaign.

Yet, every single day your communication choices will impact your efforts and your personal brand. The tone and quality of your emails, voice mails and instant messages impact how colleagues or prospects engage with you. Every face-to-face communication, from one-on-one to one-on-many, offers an opportunity for you to deliver an important message. From everyday interactions to formal presentations, your communication skills help you fulfill your responsibility to lead from where you stand.

Communication as the action verb of leadership

It is your job to communicate your objectives with all the power at your command. As long as you collect those paychecks, you have a responsibility to work for the success of the organization that issues them. It's up to you to sell the goods – even when you're not so sure you'd buy them yourself.

As a young actor, I participated in a new play series at a major regional repertory theater. In this kind of workshop atmosphere, actors play a dual role. During rehearsals, they're invited to critique each script and make suggestions for improving it. But once each play opens, they're expected to give their absolute all to performing it as it is written. One of the plays in the series, by a playwright who would go on to become quite well-known, had significant problems that all the actors recognized. We pleaded with the author and the director to address these problems, but both were blind to the flaws in the work.

Emotions ran high during rehearsals; there were moments of crisis and gloom. A mordant joke circulated among the actors: "How many playwrights does it take to change a light bulb? None – it doesn't need changing!" But when the curtain went up on opening night, did we go onstage and sulk? Did we "back off" from the script we were given or, even worse, try to sabotage it with poor performances? Of course not. We did everything we could, in every performance, to make the play succeed as the playwright created it. We left it to the audience to judge the work, because that's what actors owe to every playwright and every audience.

How Can I Sell a Message I Don't Believe?

Nobody wants to stand up and rave about a product they're afraid will fail, an initiative they think is wrong-headed, or a position they find flimsy. Clients sometimes take me aside and ask some very hard questions: What if I really don't believe in this product? What if I think this initiative is misguided? What if I know I'm simply covering for somebody else's mistakes? How can I sell this message – how am I supposed to survive this presentation – when I think it's flawed? Can I duck and cover?

Get involved early to define strategy.

If you are charged with leading programs or product design, you need to get involved early to impact their destiny. Use your expert communication skills to help define the strategy. When you do, you'll minimize the number of times you feel like hedging your persuasions.

Reconsider your position with an open mind.

Luckily, the issues are not often so black and white. When your convictions are at odds with what you're being asked to communicate, it's time to take stock. Reconsider your position with an open mind. Make an effort to learn more about why the organization has embarked on an initiative you think is flawed, taken a position with which you disagree, or shipped a product you question.

Usually you can commit without compromising your values.

Let's be realistic. Most jobs and careers involve at least a few occasions when you just have to take a deep breath and do your best. You can't always limit your support to ideas and initiatives that meet your personal approval. There may be times when you have to ask yourself: Can I get on board without compromising my

Projecting your passion is your professional responsibility.

fundamental beliefs or values? I've found that most times, in most circumstances, most people will be able to answer, "Yes."

Find Your Way to "Yes."

Victors keep
the big picture
in sight.

In the end, if you cannot effect a change, or perhaps you were not even heard … You still need to get on board and dedicate your passion and your skills to selling.

Leaders and persuaders who don't commit, end up saying things like "Well, they told us we need to … Corporate says we have to …" I can tell you from experience that using the *they* word will damage your credibility and diminish your power of persuasion.

If it's your job to communicate, it's your job to find your way to that "Yes" behind your message. Then, on that foundation, it's your job to build a commitment to what you are communicating and why. You will only be persuasive if you are committed.

One caveat applies.

If a wrong-headed initiative is truly a deal breaker – if it goes outside the boundaries, is so counter to the culture, stupid, or perhaps unethical – and you have done what you can to help others see the light and they don't … Well, perhaps it is time to make another job your job, Bob.

Once You're on Board... Stoke Your Commitment.

Great persuaders and presenters learn to stoke their commitment so they can present their programs and products with passion.

So don't poke holes in your own arguments.

Sometimes the problem is being too smart. I find that my most intelligent, thoughtful, and informed clients are often harder on themselves and their messages than they should be. They compulsively poke holes in their own arguments. They over-analyze the situation, the position they're taking or the announcement they're making. In the process, they lose sight of the big picture and start to hedge their commitment to the project.

And don't fixate on the flaws.

And when it comes to products – face it – we all know too much. We know what was cut from the specs. We know the flaws. We know what the 2.0 version will do that the 1.0 version will not. We forget that even the 1.0 product is cutting-edge and will delight many people who will appreciate this solution.

It's your job, Bob. Never let this knowledge diminish how you project your passion for the product. Never let it sneak into your persuasion. If you do, your audience will smell it and you will lose.

Using your power of persuasion – it's your professional responsibility.

Victor or Victim? - That's Up to You.

When you're speaking or persuading in public, you have a choice: you can be a victor or a victim. What I want to emphasize here is that this is a choice you make – or rather, a series of choices. Staring at you from the page, this truth may seem obvious. But time and again, I've seen people make choices that set them up to be victims rather than victors. And more often than not, they are unaware of those choices.

Victors are Confident.

This may seem obvious, even banal. There's a saying that's been making the rounds: "Whether you believe you will succeed or you will fail, you are right." Sounds like the mother of all self-help mantras, doesn't it? And then there's our media culture, where sports are supremely important and we get to see athletes "up close and personal" – probably more than we would like. From boxers to baseball players, we hear plenty of "psyching myself up," "finding the flow," or "imagining victory."

But strip away all the hype, and there's still plenty of truth in the clichés about confidence. Superior athletes and great competitors in every walk of life grasp it intuitively. Most of us have to learn it, and understand the bearing it has on our power of persuasion. It is this: The more confident you are, the better you will perform. When you're confident in front of an audience, you're relaxed but alert. You breathe more deeply and evenly. Oxygen fills your lungs and flows freely to your muscles, giving you more vocal and physical energy, and to your brain, enabling you to think more clearly. In full command of all your resources as a speaker, you are capable of performing at your peak.

At the other extreme is what's called stage fright, which is actually a severe case of under-confidence. In a person afflicted with stage fright, breathing becomes rapid and shallow; the heart races and so does the mind. The person feels ill because he is. Physically and mentally debilitated, such a person doesn't have a chance of performing at his peak; just getting through the ordeal at hand is challenge enough.

In later chapters, I talk about being nervous (which is not unhealthy – far from it) and preparing your body and voice for speaking in public. What I want to do here is make you aware of some of the most common choices every speaker must make – choices between victor and victim, choices that will either bolster or undermine your confidence.

Don't buy into negative perceptions.

I've worked with and observed presenters who buy into negative perceptions about their company or industry or profession. People in technology who are troubled by the distrust of customers or competitors. People in healthcare who feel that, somehow, they are personally to blame for the costs and complexities of modern healthcare. People in pharmaceuticals who feel tainted by direct-to-

You make choices that impact the outcome of your persuasion.

consumer drug advertising. In every case, by buying into negative perceptions, they have lost confidence and their power of persuasion.

Don't dwell on the flaws or limitations of your company's new product or service. Don't lose your way in a thicket of "on-the-other-hand," "yeah-but," and "what-if." Get psyched, go out there and tell your story with confidence! That's what victors do.

Make Victor Choices.

Finally, as a public speaker, you will often have some very practical choices to make, both before and after you take the floor. These are victor-victim choices.

Victims agree to talk about issues or answer questions that are outside their expertise. Victims cut corners on preparation and rehearsals. Victims don't bother to visit the site of their presentation – the "set" for their performance – ahead of time; or if they do, they're too polite to ask that the room set-up be changed to improve sight lines or seating configuration. Victims get flustered by microphones and unfamiliar equipment. Instead of making sure that everything is organized for their success, victims "let come what may," which only drives up the chances they will fail. Instead of demanding the attention of every person in the room, victims allow audience members to talk or escape to their smartphones, iPads or laptops.

Make Success Inevitable.

Start by knowing you're going to win!

Your production calendar begins as soon as you find out about your presentation. You control every activity you take up until the final moment. Take steps to guarantee your success:

- Rehearse
- Before your presentation, engage with and "take the temperature" of your audience
- Walk the stage before the presentation
- Test all the equipment
- Practice your presentation with and without the technology (which may fail)
- Prepare an abbreviated presentation in case of a schedule change
- Anticipate issues and prepare solutions!

The Victor's Bill of Rights

- I have the right to speak about what I know best and to speak about what moves me.

- I have a right to the time and resources I need to prepare and rehearse prior to a presentation.

- I have a right to coaching and feedback as I prepare for a presentation.

- I have the right to refuse last-minute changes and requests that will undermine my preparation and confidence.

- I have the right to control the presentation environment. This includes (but is not limited to) the right to be comfortable with any technology that will be part of my presentation, to have the microphone at the proper height, and to ask for a glass of water.

- I have the right to be heard. This includes the right to demand an audience's attention.

- I have the right to pause to collect my thoughts, correct myself, or repeat anything I think the audience might have missed.

- I have the right not to answer a question or respond to a comment.

- I have a right to answer their question with my message.

- I have the right to be confident.

- I have the right to succeed.

You have control over your success!

Exercises: Uncovering Your Passion

Craft Your Statement of Professional Passion.

Sit down with a colleague or turn on a tape recorder and answer the following questions:

What is your professional passion?

Why is your work important? Why does it matter to the world, and why does it matter to you? What do you love about what you do?

When the going gets tough, what keeps you going?

When things are not going well, how do you feel? Why do you put up with the hassles and the headaches?

✔

Are you …

A problem
solver?

An innovator?

A people
person?

Tell the Story of Your Most Pride-filled Moment.

Sit down with a colleague or turn on a tape recorder and tell the story of the most pride-filled moment in your profession.

And by story, I mean: "Once upon a time – and then one day – and because of that – and I'll never forget the moment when." Be as specific as possible in describing and relating the circumstances and emotions around this story of this memorable moment.

What are the underlying themes in this story?

Is this a story of innovation? Problem solving? Teamwork?

Jot down the story as you may wish to tell it in the future to inspire a team, recruit a like-minded professional, profile yourself and your work, or interview for a job.

Chapter 2

Listen Up!

Effective Listening is Key to Winning Persuasions.

During my first year of formal training as a professional actor, the focus was not on how well students talked when we were on stage, but on how well we listened. We would act out scenes together, and then the instructor would critique our "performances." I put that word in quotes because, in fact, we heard almost nothing about the way we had delivered our own lines; instead, we got extensive feedback on how well we had listened when the other actor was talking. I'm sure I wasn't the only student asking himself, "This is acting?" But, though some egos got bruised along the way, eventually we absorbed the truth and importance of our instructor's approach. In theater parlance, we were learning that acting is the art of "being in the moment," and you simply can't do that if you don't listen to the other actors onstage. More fundamentally, we were learning that all communication is a transaction – a transaction between people – and what happens on the listening end is just as important as what happens on the talking end.

The Power of Persuasion is largely a matter of projecting who you are and what you want to say, clearly and forcefully, and most of this book focuses on helping you do that. But developing your listening skills is also an essential part of your preparation as a communicator. For one thing, preparation for a speech or presentation often involves gathering information from other people. With good listening skills, you will literally hear more when others talk, because good listening encourages good communication.

WIIFM - "What's in it For Me?"

Just as important to your preparation, it's your job to learn what you can about the audience in advance. What do they expect to hear? What do they want to hear? What might engage them, challenge them, motivate them? "WIIFM" – short for "What's in it for me?" – is the siren song no audience can resist. But in order to create that seductive music, you have to be a good listener.

What's in it for your audience?

How to be a Better Listener

On his way to a guaranteed laugh, one of my acting teachers once said, "The key to great acting is being truthful. [pause] And if you can fake that, you've got it made."

The wisdom behind the joke applies as much to listening as it does to talking. Faking genuine interest almost always backfires. But that doesn't mean you can't develop habits that help you improve your listening.

For some people, good listening comes naturally; they simply have a knack for listening in a caring and heartfelt manner, attuned not only to the words but also to the emotions of the speaker. For the rest of us, good listening requires focus, intention, and training – just as I learned in acting school. Every parent of young children knows that human beings decide when they want to listen (and when they don't). We can also control *how* we listen, which means we can ensure that we listen well. It just takes a bit of work – a combination of will, awareness, and technique.

In one of the most popular Power of Persuasion workshops, I engage groups in various listening games and exercises. The exercises require people to use their bodies in the communication process; what gets everyone laughing and enjoying themselves – and makes them better, more aware listeners – is finding that their ears and their brains go where their bodies lead. Following is a summary of what these listening workshops demonstrate.

Engage Your Body: Lean In.

Body language speaks silently but eloquently; moment by moment, it expresses how well you are listening. Good listening requires body language that enhances rather than hampers the transaction between you and the person speaking. So it's important to be aware of productive and non-productive body language and to practice using those that serve you best. The basics do's and don'ts include:

Do:

- Lean in slightly toward the speaker, it makes you more present
- Keep an open posture
- Affirm by nodding your head occasionally

Don't:

- Play the withholder
- Sit back in judgment or cross your arms
- Fidget, tap your foot, click your pen, check your watch, and so forth

Combine genuine interest with good listening behaviors.

Making Eye Contact

Eye contact is a crucial element of communication. This is what our parents were trying to teach us when they told us to "look the man in the eye." The matter is a little more complicated than our parents might have known. Cultural anthropologists have made us aware that there are marked cultural variations around the issue of eye contact. In an era of globalization, anyone who interacts face-to-face with people from non-Western societies must be sensitive to those variations. Nevertheless, in North America the generally accepted practice is to engage people's eyes when you are listening.

Yes, but how much eye contact is appropriate? I'm certainly not recommending you lock eyes with everyone with whom you engage. Anyone who has been subjected to this form of "listening" knows how uncomfortable it can be. On the other hand, the proverbial saying "the eyes are the window to the soul" reminds us that people's eyes often tell us how they feel about what they're saying, and that's an important part of all communication.

Don't over-think it.

When listening to someone, simply engage his or her eyes enough to "check in and check up" – to let them know that you are following them. By engaging their eyes, you have the additional benefit of tuning into the emotion and commitment behind their words.

Checking for Understanding

Checking to make sure we've heard correctly is an excellent way to ensure we're listening carefully. Reiterate their message in your own words using simple phrases like "So what I'm hearing you say is …" or "Let me be sure I understand you …" This gives the speaker a chance to confirm or correct your understanding and to clarify their intention. It also assures them you are a good listener, and that makes them want to keep talking to you.

Taking Notes

If you know you're not a great listener, you may want to take notes. You probably want to ask permission, but you'll find people are very respectful. Taking notes shows you value the person's insights and opinions. Checking for understanding plus note-taking will make you a better listener.

Empathetic Listening and "Why" Questions

Listening happens on many levels. Some people listen for the facts, focusing on the words and the literal detail. Others have a special talent for what I call empathetic

Eyes are the windows into the soul...

of those you are hoping to persuade.

listening: they're able to connect not just with what someone is saying but also with how the speaker feels about what he or she is saying. Then there are those who ask themselves a series of "why" questions while they listen: "Why is this person saying that? … What's really going on here? … What's behind that comment? … What's the real story?"

Empathetic listeners and people who listen with the "why" questions working in the background of their minds get my vote as "best of class" listeners. They often glean information from their interactions others do not – nuances of fact or feeling that can open up whole new perspectives on events or issues, as well as hidden agendas, unspoken resistance, and other obstacles to progress or change.

✔

People who ask "why" usually find out more.

When you're lucky enough to run into empathetic listeners, observe them closely and try to emulate their techniques – provided you can do so genuinely. And try to cultivate the habit of asking "why" questions when listening to others. These two listening styles can make you a more effective listener.

What Kind of Listener are You?

To understand the importance of good listening – and what kind of listener you are – you can start by being aware of how other people listen. Two archetypes define the extremes of listening styles. Although most of us fall somewhere in between, we usually share at least some of the characteristics of both extremes, at least some of the time.

Withholders

These are the people who give back nothing – zero, zilch, nada – when you talk to them. They often sit with arms crossed, their expression blank if not slightly troubled. It's easy to feel that they're sitting in judgment of you – if they haven't already found you guilty! Speaking to them is like sending information into a black hole. We've all met withholders, probably more often than we'd like.

Some, I believe, are misguided by the belief that all communications are about power and status; in withholding, they've found their favorite intimidation technique. Others, I'm sure, don't engage in withholding on purpose; they simply come from a background that predisposed them to this kind of expressionless listening. And many people who aren't ordinarily withholders will retreat into this listening style in threatening or stressful situations.

Identifying a withholder is key to dealing with them.

Whatever their reasons, withholders make it tough on the rest of us. Their lack of response can be extremely frustrating and stressful; it can take us off our game, which is precisely what some withholders seem to have in mind. Our inner monologue goes wild: "Why is this interaction going so badly? Does he think I'm full of it? Do I have spinach in my teeth? Maybe if I try harder, or change my message, I can get some kind of response."

After an encounter with a withholder, it's easy to feel you've failed miserably in gathering any meaningful information. That's why it's important to be able to identify a withholder when you deal with one – you'll know that your apparent failure to connect is not your fault. By sabotaging communications, withholders really shortchange no one but themselves.

Check in with withholders.

Clients often ask me how they should respond to this extreme style of listening. I suggest continual "checking" with withholders – that is, ask them frequently if they understand what you're saying, what they think of what you've said, if they agree or disagree, and what they might add. It's also a good idea to turn some of your statements into questions that require a response. When you feel you can risk it, come right out and tell withholders that you need more feedback. Tell them since you're not sure what they're thinking, you're concerned that you're not communicating effectively.

Withholders tend to be poor communicators.

If you think you are a withholder, I strongly recommend that you make an effort to change your ways. Withholders aren't just poor listeners; they tend to be poor communicators as well. They get much less information, and much less help, from interactions with people, and they often end up delivering the wrong message.

Gushers

Gushers appear to think of listening as a vigorous physical challenge, a matter of continuous head nodding, endless "ums" and "ahs," and frequent interruptions. Maybe they believe that they're making it easier and more comfortable for us to communicate with them. But more often than not, their ostentatious, hyperactive manner of listening distracts us from communicating effectively. Continually interrupted, prevented from finishing a thought, even actively encouraged to go off course, we may find that talking with a gusher is even more unsettling than dealing with a withholder.

Ask gushers to help you keep your train of thought.

When you deal with gushers, it can be difficult to get them to minimize the affirmations. There just aren't many ways to tell people that they're being too nice. But you can get them to stop the interruptions. Tell them that you "really want to get this right" and their interruptions are causing you to lose your train of thought.

Ask them to wait to ask questions – even to jot down notes – so that you can engage in dialogue when you "finish laying out the background."

Is there spinach in my teeth?

Does he think I'm full of it?

Oh I see... he's a withholder.

Am I showing
how well I
listen – or am
I derailing the
speaker?

Excessive gushing diminishes authority.

And if you think you are a gusher, take stock – you would do well to develop another style of listening. Just as the withholder's style may serve to elevate his or her status and authority, gushing is sure to do the opposite for you. During many executive coaching sessions, I've had to ask the client to back off on the gushing. Excessive nodding, prodding, and affirmation diminish a person's authority. More likely than not, it will mark you as someone who is "not a leader."

Know Your Style and How to Adapt It.

Knowing your style is the key, so you can modulate it as necessary. Wherever each of us fits on the scale between withholders and gushers, we can borrow elements from both in order to become better listeners.

For instance, used in moderation, gushing with someone who needs encouragement will allow him or her to gain confidence, open up, and communicate more fully and more clearly.

Conversely, some people we encounter need to feel that they have our complete focus in order to communicate well; they'll communicate better if we rein back our responses in the manner of the withholder.

Listen Before You Persuade.

Most of my client engagements are about more than a single speech. They are about an extended communications campaign. Like any such effort, a communications campaign takes careful planning, thinking, and listening.

In undertaking such a campaign – even in preparing for a one-time presentation – you may think you know what your key objectives are. You may think you understand all the obstacles. But do you? Again, all communication is a transaction between speaker and listener.

Your audiences will bring their own ideas, thoughts, and feelings to every meeting, every presentation, and every event. Unless you understand their point of view, their concerns and prejudices and fears, their current levels of understanding and resistance regarding your objectives – unless you understand all of that, you can't plan a persuasive presentation, you can't craft effective messages, you can't even be sure you've defined your objective correctly and completely.

Put your ear to the ground and listen.

That's why I urge my clients to go on a listening tour before preparing a presentation or planning a campaign. Internally, your listening tour may simply be a stroll through the work site to engage important people and find out about their current perceptions and concerns. Externally, it might mean more.

A recent client took the listening tour exercise very seriously. New to his leadership position but slated to give a keynote address at an industry conference attended by his most important customers and partners, he actually got on the airplane and met with six of his most important constituents. When he returned from the trip, he had a whole new perspective on his keynote.

Know Your Obstacles Before You Persuade.

In my practice I'm often coaching leaders responsible for driving change. In their communications they must inspire people to do something new, different and often scary. What you don't want to hear or sense from your audience is "Phooey!"

phoo • ey (**foo**-ee)

interjection; informal exclamation

1. — used to express disbelief, disappointment, or a strong dislike for something.

Phooey!

That is why it is important to listen for the obstacles to change.

The mnemonic FFUUEE (Phooey) may help you as you consider these obstacles to change:

- Fear

- Fairness

- Understanding (Lack of)

- Urgency (Lack of)

- Entitlement

- Exhaustion

Listen for issues of Fear.

Many times the real obstacle to your persuasion is fear. Your audience may be fearful of change and all that it entails – new methods, new people, and new technology. While understanding the logic of what's new would seem to be most important, it's the fear of the new and unknown that creates the resistance.

Those who listen for and recognize fear will be better prepared to persuade by addressing the fear with simple solutions – air cover, training, clarity on how the change will impact schedule and work flow.

Effective persuasion requires understanding the audience point of view.

Listen for fear of risk-taking. Often your great idea will put another's reputation on the line. You need to address the fear that your failure or your success will impact them.

Effective persuasions inspire urgent action!

Listen for Fairness issues.

Fairness issues tend to be most prevalent in leadership communications. Leaders with a compelling vision will often ask people to do more than they thought possible. They will ask people to work in new ways with different people at different intensities. Don't be surprised when your compelling vision meets resistance as being unfair to one or more constituencies.

If you are leading teams, keep in mind that you may not always be able to offer fairness. Instead you may be best served to call out the differences and thank those who are doing the heavy lifting to drive success. Over the long term, your goal as a leader should be to spread out the pain while making sure everyone enjoys the gain.

Listen for a lack of Understanding.

Perhaps the audience simply does not understand the problem, the technology, the context, the risk or myriad other important facts that would help them see your point of view. If you listen for and recognize a lack of understanding, you will likely create a persuasion with a rich educational element. Enlightening those who simply did not understand removes barriers and creates an audience willing to come along on your persuasion.

Listen for a lack of Urgency.

It is very possible that as a persuader, you will do what you need to help people understand. You may even address their fear and fairness issues. This does not guarantee you will win the persuasion. Passive or soft agreement is not going to get you the gold medal.

Your goal is to make your topic one of the top three urgent ideas or initiatives for your audience. Your goal is to create an urgency that makes them jump up and pitch in. So test the sense of urgency in your audiences ahead of time. Listen. Can you hear how soft or how sharp their interest and support may be?

In later chapters we'll investigate how to use persuasion tools to intensify urgency.

Listen for Entitlement.

The term "entitlement" refers to a notion or belief that one is deserving of some particular reward or benefit. Entitlement can creep into the culture of organizations and lead to serious resistance to new ideas and change. It often plays out as passive or passive aggressive resistance to your persuasion.

In my experience, I have found it very difficult to persuade the entitled. I recommend that if possible, you simply "manage" the entitled while focusing your power of persuasion on those on the leading edge of your audience.

Listen for Exhaustion.

As a leader driving change, it is up to you to manage the resources at hand. And one of your most important resources is the energy of the team. Take the long view and try to recognize the rhythm and cadence of leadership. Listen for the exhaustion so that you craft a campaign to inspire and energize.

Listening While Presenting

Listening is a critical skill during interactive presentations. Panel discussions, conferences, team meetings, sessions with the media, and so forth – forums like these require you to listen as well as speak. And how well you listen informs how well—and how persuasively—you speak.

If you listen, you can hear an audience asking you to change it up.

Even when you're behind the podium and doing all the talking, you must listen to your audience. Just as it is for actors on stage, listening is the most effective means we have of conveying genuine interest in other people. And it is vital to convey genuine interest in those you wish to persuade. It will enable you to command their attention with a presentation energy that says, "I care about what you are hearing and right now, in this moment, I am listening to and attentive to your reaction."

Be alert to what the audience is telling you.

Even as you're talking, be alert to the things your audience is telling you. Think of it as a form of instant polling to help you make course corrections in your presentation on the fly. We've all sat through presentations, from classes to conferences, where some misguided speaker droned on and on, as the shuffling of feet and paper, the shifting in seats and clearing of throats grew toward a crescendo. Remember how embarrassed you felt for that speaker, or how disdainful?

An audience will tell you when you need to move on to a new topic, change your position on the stage, add variety to your vocal style – anything to recapture their attention. Later chapters introduce various ways to do that. But in order to know when to put those techniques in action – Listen up!

Exercises: Listening Skills

Listening for Understanding

It's best to have a stopwatch when doing this exercise. Sit with a partner and have him or her answer, in 5 to 7 minutes, the following questions about a current or planned communications campaign:

- What's the "lay of the land" – that is, the situation of the organization you seek to influence?

- What are the major issues you need to address or initiatives you need to drive through your communications campaign?

- What are the major obstacles to success?

- How do you plan to overcome those obstacles?

You must hear
what is being
said.

Play it Back and Get a Grade.

In two or three minutes, play back the key elements of what you heard. Ask your partner how completely and accurately you heard what you were told.

Now Switch Roles.

If your partner is willing, switch roles. This exercise can serve both of you in two ways: it can help you develop your listening skills, and it can also give you an opportunity to plan and develop a communications campaign.

Listening for Obstacles (FFUUEE!)

Choose a current initiative or a project that is real to your success right now. Think about the people you will need to persuade in order to achieve that success.

- Fear: Are there fear issues?

- Fairness: Are there fairness issues?

- Lack of Understanding: What is it your audience does not understand?

- Urgency: Is my project on the front burner with these people? What is the sense of urgency?

- Entitlement: Are there issues of entitlement?

- Exhaustion: Do you have an accurate read on the energy and spirit of the team?

Chapter 3

The Vision Thing

The Power of a Visionary Leader

vi-sion n. 1. The sense of sight: eyesight. 2. Unusual discernment; intelligent foresight; a leader of vision.

Vision. It separates the leaders from the worker bees.

It's no accident that we describe a person with vision as both inspired and inspiring. That's what vision does: it breathes the power of persuasion into the person who gives voice to it, and the force of conviction into the people who hear it. But, like charisma, vision is elusive or intimidating or both. Skeptics may think of vision as a cliché, or as something pompous or flaky or phony (at least until they encounter someone who has it). The skeptics' view, I suspect, is just sour grapes.

For them, as for many of us, vision is one of those "grand" ideals that seems beyond our abilities – or our responsibilities. We recognize its extraordinary power when we experience it in others. But if we're asked to describe our own vision, we start to squirm.

"Martin Luther King Jr. had vision – that's what made him great," we're likely to think. "The CEO has vision – that's why she's the CEO. But me – with a vision? Anything I came up with would just sound hollow, and I'd look like a fool."

Building a Compelling Vision

But vision is not beyond any of us, and part of your preparation as a speaker or presenter is to cultivate a vision of your own. Whether you're cynical about "the vision thing" or intimidated by some inflated notion of what vision is and who has it, I suggest you stick a pin in your idea of vision, let some of the air out of it, and shrink it down to everyday size. Then start looking around. The elements of a coherent, compelling vision lie all around you, whatever your profession or position.

Look Up.

To have vision – to see – you have to open your eyes and look. You have to look far and you have to look near. Hunkered down as we are in the day-to-day of our jobs, it's all too easy for most of us, most of the time, to lose sight of "the big picture." Leaders are people who make it a regular practice to raise their heads and scan the horizon. There, after all, is where the big picture – ideas, trends, possibilities – is to be seen.

Drill Down.

Drilling down can be just as important as looking around, because the full meaning and import of things are rarely to be found on the surface. Think of yourself as a detective sifting the evidence. Get used to asking yourself and others, "What's really going on here, and why?" This habit of mind, also typical of leaders, will give you a depth of understanding that goes beneath the surface – the kind of insight a compelling vision is built on.

Provide Insight over Information.

Authority, vision, leadership: when speaking in public, none of these is a matter of showing off how much you know, but of how much you understand. We've all sat through presentations made up of one PowerPoint slide after another, all crammed with "facts," while the speaker plodded along in a tedious recitation of information we could just as easily have read in the printed hand-out. Who wants to listen to a data download or be blown over by a fire hose of information?

Facts and data enrich the story. They are not the story.

Information is important. Writing teachers speak of the power of illustrative details – the scarlet dress, the million-dollar heist, the shudder of the ship. In an effective speech or presentation, facts and data serve as illustrative details: they enrich the "story," make it vivid, and convince us that it is true. But they are not the story itself.

Don't tell them "What."

Tell them "Why."

Tell them... What does this mean?

Every audience wants to hear more than a recitation of the facts; they want to hear what you make of the facts. It's not enough to tell them, "the data is trending in this or that direction" – they want to hear your insights about why and what it all means. Anyone can tell us what's happening. An insightful, persuasive speaker – one that we want to listen to and agree with – tells us why. That is the vision thing.

History as the Gateway to the Future

Understand the
past to unlock
the promise of
the future.

As expressed by the dictionary definition at the head of this chapter, vision is a matter of "intelligent foresight." That's why daring to predict the future is important. But vision – and the wherewithal to predict the future – often rests on knowing and understanding the past.

> Paul Saffo is a highly influential Silicon Valley technology thought leader. His current endeavor, DISCERN, is an information analytics company specializing in institutional research and foresight. He helps companies plan for the future and has won the trust of major businesses and government agencies around the world, including 3M, Intel, and the U.S. Postal Service. Understandably, the press likes to refer to Mr. Saffo as a "futurist." But it's a label he dislikes. As he has said, the secret of his success is not that he is a futurist but that he is an historian. His forecasting rests on his ability to recognize and understand the constants, not the novelties, in the evolution of technology, industry, and society.

If you want to impress an audience as a person of vision, you could do worse than follow Paul Saffo's example. Again, any time you speak or present in public, you are projecting yourself as an authority. You owe it to yourself and to your audience to know your stuff, and that includes the history of your business or industry, the technical innovations that led to your new product, and the analytics and relevant data of your profession or field you want to influence.

Only by understanding the past will you really be qualified to recognize, much less announce, the milestones of today or the promises of the future. Just as the dictionary says, vision is intelligent – which means, among other things, informed foresight.

Dare to Predict Changes and Trends.

There is prodigious power in prediction. In my work, I get many opportunities to observe people as they watch presentations, and I have seen it again and again: an audience will literally lean forward in their seats when a speaker says something like "By this time next year, we'll see that ..." or "I believe that three years from now ..." No wonder the leaders who capture the most attention are the ones who dare to build predictions into their presentations.

There are worse things than being wrong.

After all, when you make a prediction, what's the worst thing that can happen? You'll be wrong. By then, chances are, no one will remember your prediction. Besides, there are worse things than being wrong. When I work with leaders, I advise them that there's far more downside risk in being seen as someone with no idea, or afraid to say what the future holds.

What trends and issues are going to drive your industry in the next two years or three or five? How will behavior change with the introduction of your company's new innovation? What will the jury conclude when you've finished presenting the evidence? How will this reorganization impact your employees and your customers? Dare to predict. If you've done your homework and thought through the facts and issues, you'll probably be right. In the meantime, you'll surely be regarded by your audience as a person with a strong point of view.

Futurecasting puts a vision into words.

Futurecasting

To create and communicate a compelling vision, one of the best approaches involves telling the story of the future. This is why I take many clients through a process I call aspirational storytelling, or futurecasting. While storytelling as a multi-purpose technique is discussed in detail in Chapter 6, I introduce aspirational storytelling here because it's such a great way to create a vision and put it into words.

Describe the Future in Vivid and Specific Detail.

The goal of futurecasting is to describe what life will look like and feel like, in vivid and specific detail, when your idea, your strategy, or your mission has come to fruition. For example, you might describe a day in the life of your customers as they use, experience, and benefit from your product. Or tell the story of a week in the life of your management team once they've come together around a plan for organizational growth and development.

Your story of the future can take many forms. Martin Luther King Jr.'s classic "I have a dream" speech is a tried and true model. Another compelling approach is to tell your story from the point of view of the future, looking back on the present moment as if it were the past: "Back in 2014 we made three key decisions, and on that foundation we have built the company that dominates our industry today ..."

Some examples:

> In healthcare, clients have used aspirational storytelling to paint pictures of the use of telecommunication and information technologies in order to provide clinical health care at a distance.

> *

> A PR agency created the story of a high stakes situation where the client deftly navigated difficult political waters, then revealed what was going on behind the scenes to facilitate that success.

*

Technology executives have produced a detailed "day in the life" scenario of a professional enjoying cloud-enabled access to personal data, music, movies, and games while on the road.

*

A social networking client describes how his company will mine "big data" and personalize advertising offers to customers.

Futurecasting can be the start of a strategic plan.

Aspirational storytelling can facilitate more than message development – far more. It often serves as a form of strategic planning, because you can't describe a future of success without explaining how you will create that success. For leaders and management teams, painting a picture of the future is often the catalyst for coming to grips with what the organization must do to get there.

You've painted the picture. Now tell them how to get there.

That's why, when I coach leaders, I often begin with aspirational storytelling. But again, vision is not for leaders only. A magical elixir compounded of insight, aspiration, and determination, vision can make leaders of us all.

Exercise: Vision

Practice intelligent foresight.

Look Up!

In this exercise, take some time to look up. Be the historian, the archeologist, the detective. Looking at history and emerging trends brings you the power of visionary thinking. Visionary thinking is persuasive.

Scan the horizon.

Ask yourself:

Where have we come from? Where are we going?

What are the emerging trends in your industry? How will they impact you?

What do you see as the key data points worth exploring for future impact?

Envision the future.

Most important, how can you take advantage of these trends to innovate new products or services and win in the marketplace?

Chapter 4

Building Message Mantra

Successful Persuasion – Compelling Messages

We tend to think of talking as a "lesser" form of communication. After all, our days are filled with conversation, but occasions for "formal" speaking are few and far between. For important communications, such as those in business and professional life, we may tend to believe it's necessary to "put it in writing."

There's no question that the printed word has a certain authority. And writing is often an essential means both to discovering what we think and to organizing our thoughts.

So why do I suggest that the spoken word is king?

We're awash in documentation; we can't read it all.

Think about your desk and your computer desktop at work. If you're like most people, you're awash in documents of all kinds, sent to you by people who want to inform or influence you, solicit your ideas or share their own. Think, too, how many emails you send every week, how many plans, proposals, and reports you write in a month or a year.

And then consider all the times you've distributed a written plan or proposal – even something as simple as an agenda – prior to a meeting. The idea is that the attendees will review the document before they attend, right? But as the meeting gets underway, you soon come to the unsettling conclusion that no one has read what you wrote.

Or, if you've ever given a media interview, think about what was quoted in the story. It wasn't the background documents you gave to the reporters to educate and inform them – it's what you said during the interview that got into print. The fact is, people just don't read much anymore. Chances are, what you say about a plan, a proposal, or a report is going to have far more influence than the document itself.

The spoken word is king.

Say everything
out loud before
you commit it
to paper.

Start with the medium you will use to present: The spoken word.

And yet, when getting ready for a presentation, many people spend the lion's share of their preparation time on the written word – creating background documents, outlining what they want to cover, writing PowerPoint slides. They spend little time – even no time at all – actually speaking aloud what they want to say when the moment comes that they're on their feet and everyone is looking at them expectantly. They go into battle like a soldier who's spent the night before polishing his boots instead of cleaning his rifle.

As you go about discovering and developing your message, it's essential that you use the same medium you will use to present: the spoken word. That means saying out loud everything you will say in your presentation before you commit it to paper or PowerPoint.

Define the messages.

What do you want your presentation to communicate? If you're like most people, you'll have far too much to say – a fire hose of information, a laundry list of ideas. That's OK. The point is to tease out everything you need to say based on the information you gleaned in your "listening tour."

And then refine.

That's the beginning of the message development process, but it's far from the end. First you gather your ideas. Next, you have to refine them. Just as you must painstakingly draft, redraft, and edit a written document to make it as effective and persuasive as it can be, you need to do the same with any spoken word presentation.

By bringing up the analogy to writing, I do not mean to suggest that at this stage you are outlining your presentation. This chapter and the process it describes are not about structuring a presentation – that comes later. The objective here is to focus your thinking, your ideas, and your language on the goal you want to achieve, the ideas you want your audience to remember, the thing or things you want them to do.

Reduce the Sauce and Prioritize Content.

Your first task is to take each important idea and condense it to its core, its most powerful but complete essence. I call this reducing the sauce. If you've ever made a risotto or created a fine bordelaise or similar sauce, you'll understand the point of my analogy: less is more. In cooking, a sauce acquires complexity, subtlety, depth, and power as it's reduced until the critical moment when it reaches perfection. By the same token, a cook can weaken or spoil a sauce by reducing it too much.

Maximize power without sacrificing clarity or completeness.

The same is true of a spoken message. You have to go through a process of reducing the sauce to maximize the persuasive power of a message without sacrificing its clarity and completeness.

Consider the first message the health food company leader arrived at during her discovery process:

> *By straying from our core strength, we have awakened sleeping giants who are gearing up to compete ferociously with us.*

While it's dramatic and vivid – "watch out for those sleeping giants!" – in this form, the message is long and cumbersome. In fact, it sounds suspiciously like two messages:

> *We have strayed from our core strength.* AND

> *We have awakened sleeping giants who are gearing up to compete ferociously with us.*

The second idea is a consequence of the first. To reduce the sauce, my client focused on the first idea. But something was missing – just what was the core strength she was talking about? That, of course, had found its way into other messages on her list. "Customer service" was the seasoning she needed to add to the sauce while reducing it:

> *We have strayed from our core strength: customer service.*

This formulation was missing the element of "so what?" – the sense of what was at stake – conveyed by the threat of the "sleeping giants." So she experimented with ways of restoring that element, enriching the sauce while reducing it. Eventually, she arrived at this:

> *Where we used to be strong, in customer service, we are now weak – and vulnerable.*

This was short, complete, dramatic, memorable – in a word, powerful. It also gave my client a foundation to build on as she took other messages on her list, reduced the sauce with each one, and put them together to build her case for reinventing the company through "disciplined entrepreneurship."

Experiment to reduce each message to its essence.

Reducing the sauce is a process of trial and error, experimentation, iteration and reiteration. The idea is to try out various words and phrases, formulations, and approaches for making each key point. But remember: the over-arching goal is to reduce each message to its essence. Doing that will force you to be more clear, concise, and persuasive.

Organize, prioritize and reduce a firehose of information.

You can always restore a word or two to save the sauce.

As a rule, shorter is better, but there are limits to this rule. Like sentences, messages come in various forms: simple, compound, complex, and compound complex. As with a risotto, you can spoil a message by going too far with your reduction. Fortunately, when you're preparing a presentation, you can always go back to a previous iteration, or restore a word or an idea, to save the sauce.

✔

Three is the
magic number.

The Rule of Three

From the seven days of creation to *The Seven Habits of Highly Effective People*, seven is a number that has always captivated the human intellect and imagination. Apparently, seven is also the capacity of the human memory. For example, I've read that the basic paradigm for telephone numbers – 123-4567 – is based on the fact that the average person is capable of reliably remembering a sequence of seven digits and no more.

Maybe it's the supposed magic of seven that inspired the many clients I've worked with who wanted to base their presentations on seven messages. Without exception, I have discouraged them from doing so.

> A friend of mine once told me about an executive speech he attended on "seven secrets to success" in the grocery business. As they left the presentation, he asked his wife what she thought of the speech.
>
> "Boring, for sure," she replied.
>
> "What about the so-called seven secrets?" he asked. "Did any of them resonate with you?"
>
> She paused. "To tell you the truth, I can't remember any of them. Can you?"
>
> My friend remembered three, which is exactly what I would have expected, and what every effective speaker knows. That's because when it comes to the messages in a spoken presentation, three is truly the magic number. Not seven … not five … three.

Three is memorable.

People can easily keep track of and remember things in threes: three ideas, three examples, three milestones, and so forth. In fact, we humans love to group things in threes and we seem to learn things best that way: red, white, and blue … faith, hope, and charity … readin', writin', and 'rithmetic … and all the rest.

Three is dramatic.

It's no accident that classic dramatic structure, as common in TV sitcoms as it is in opera, is based on the three-act format. Act One establishes the characters and situation; in Act Two the situation becomes more complicated and the tension builds; in Act Three the situation is resolved and the tension is released. In fact, every good story has three parts – beginning, middle, end – and so do most good speeches.

Three works.

Dramatic, engaging, and memorable, the rule of three works in politics, in strategic planning, in describing product features and benefits. And it works like gangbusters in speeches and presentations – both as an overall structural design and as the true magic number for your key messages.

Building Three Key Messages

So your next step in the message development process is to get to three – three messages that will bring your audience to understand what you want them to understand, believe what you want them to believe, and do what you want them to do.

Begin by listing your seven or more messages on a white board or piece of paper. Next, make an effort to bundle or categorize the messages on your list. Consider each one, asking yourself what, if anything, it has in common with others. Can you combine any of your messages? Can you bundle two or more into a higher-level category? Are some of them secondary to others – as premises, proof points, reasons why or implications of? If so, set them aside to use later, when you'll be filling out the substance of your presentation.

Sometimes seven points really boils down to three.

Keep combining and bundling your messages until you reduce the number to three main messages that will serve as the basis of your presentation.

> To return to the example of the health food company executive, she distilled her laundry list of messages to these three:

> 1. *We need to refocus on our core strength: customer service.*

> 2. *We need to measure and reward ourselves based on our success.*

> 3. *We need to redefine our roles and responsibilities according to a model of "disciplined entrepreneurship."*

Your Message Mantra

When you've reduced your laundry list to three essential messages, you have the basis for a presentation that your audience will be able to engage with, care about, keep track of, and – most important of all – remember when they go on their merry way.

Or will they?

In our high-speed, media-rich, and message-saturated culture, you simply can't count on your audience to have the patience or the capacity to remember more than one message from your presentation. You have to decide what that one message is, and make it your message mantra.

What's the one key message your audience must grasp?

The one macro message the audience takes away

Your message mantra is your macro message – the one message you want your audience to take with them. It's the single idea, belief, proposal, or call to action that you'll emphasize, repeat, recast, reinvigorate, and hammer home relentlessly, over and over.

Think of someone leaving your presentation and being asked, "What did she say?" Your message mantra is the answer to that question. Another approach: I've worked with PR people who defined their message mantra by asking the question "What is the headline we want to see in print tomorrow?"

Metaphors make a powerful message mantra.

Don't be afraid of a message mantra that seems "artsy" or poetic. Many message mantras are metaphors at heart or become metaphors in the course of a presentation.

For example:

> The health food company president came up with "Go for the sweet spot" as the message mantra for her presentation to employees. She started with an idiom from sports that's become part of the language of business, "the sweet spot." She used it to describe her company's traditional core strength. Then she extended the metaphor to the company's growth opportunities … to customer service as the area where the company must improve and excel … and finally to her idea of "disciplined entrepreneurship."

> By the end of her presentation, "Go for the sweet spot" wove together her three key messages. It reminded her audience of the strengths and values that bound them together, it articulated her plan for their future success together, and it described a method for executing that plan. Like Martin Luther King Jr.'s "I have a dream," it also became a rallying cry – the ultimate achievement for a message mantra.

Here's another example of a metaphor used as a powerful message mantra.

> When developing the fundraising speech for the president of a religious studies consortium, the speechwriter found a vivid, powerful message mantra in a story the client and his staff told during our briefing session. The story concerned a philanthropist who wanted to help people affected by the Indian Ocean tsunami of December 2004. In the words of the speech:

He wanted to help restore the fisheries in the coastal villages of Sumatra. So he offered a million dollars to **put the boats back in the water**. *And the aid organization he offered the money to – they turned him down.*

Because, you see, he's Jewish – and the tsunami victims of Sumatra were mostly Muslims.

Opening with this story of a derailed effort to relieve human suffering, the speech established "putting the boats back in the water" as a symbol of what's at stake in building understanding and acceptance among diverse religious faiths. The mantra was invoked again in relation to the failures of public institutions to promote dialogue, tolerance, and healing:

In the face of so much to discuss and decide, our public discourse is failing us. The rhetoric of oversimplification has taken the place of thoughtful analysis, reasoned argument, and open dialogue … And the politics of polarization carry the day.

But that kind of rhetoric, that brand of politics doesn't resolve any disagreements or solve any problems. It doesn't move the ball forward – to say nothing of the human race. **It doesn't put any boats back in the water.**

Finally, in an inspirational call to action, the mantra stood forth as a powerful metaphor for the consortium's core mission and served as a dignified way of doing the essential work of the speech, what all non-profit institutions have to do – ask for money:

We believe it's not just possible to achieve understanding among people of different religions. If humankind is to have a peaceful future, perhaps any future at all, it is imperative that we achieve such understanding.

We are committed to **putting the boats back in the water**, *and we believe it can be done. We ask you to lend a hand.*

In the entire speech, "putting the boats back in the water" appeared only three times – four, if you take into account that it was also the title of the speech. But that was enough to unite the speech's key messages in a poignant, urgent, and memorable call to action.

A metaphor can be a very powerful message mantra.

A Note on Intentional Redundancy

"Go for the sweet spot! … Go for the sweet spot! … Go for the sweet spot!" The health food company president was relentless in repeating her message mantra, and her redundancy was entirely intentional. Many presenters worry that they'll appear to be talking down to their audience if they repeat a message mantra too often. They fear that they'll sound like a cheesy late-night TV commercial and lose credibility. On the contrary ...

Don't be afraid to drive the point home.

The audience needs redundancy to grasp what's new to them.

Remember, the ideas and information you deliver may be numbingly familiar to you, but in most cases, the content of your presentation will be entirely new to your audience. They will both need and appreciate the redundancy of an oft-repeated message mantra. Sure, some people will "get it" sooner than others. But they'll be more likely to congratulate themselves for being ahead of the pack than to blame you for making your point abundantly clear.

The mantra anchors your message for the audience.

Keep in mind, too, that your message mantra is not the whole of what you have to say. Rather, it's the anchor for everything else, the Rosetta Stone your audience will use to understand and synthesize your presentation as they're listening to it and to remember it later.

And the mantra anchors your message for you.

Finally, as shown in the examples I've described, your message mantra is an anchor for you as well as your audience. By connecting your mantra with the major issues, ideas, and themes covered in your presentation, you'll ensure that your presentation holds together. In other words, your message mantra can serve you in structuring, organizing, and unifying your presentation – tasks discussed in later chapters.

Exercise: Building Message Mantra

Reduce the Sauce.

In this exercise, choose a current topic or message worth practicing. Using your watch, take two minutes to explain this topic aloud. Then reduce the sauce to get your point across in half the time, and then half again.

Reduce your message to its powerful but complete essence.

Say it in two minutes.

Reduce the sauce.

Say it in one minute.

Reduce the sauce some more.

Say it in thirty seconds.

Chapter 5

Powerbites

The Persuader's Magic Bullet

The world lives on Internet time now. As a professional communicator, you can bet that the people in your audience, accustomed to clicking and flicking instantly to what they want to read or watch or know right now, will want to hear your conclusion sooner rather than later.

The Powerbite tool transforms your power of persuasion.

Prove it. And make it snappy.

Welcome to a messaging technique that I have coined the *Powerbite*. Think of the Powerbite as a hammer – an aggressive, no-fooling-around tool for driving your message home with a few sharp, precisely-aimed blows. The Powerbite responds to the part of your listener's mind that demands, "Prove it – and make it snappy."

You're probably familiar with the "elevator pitch," an introduction or promotional spiel that's so brief it can be delivered during an elevator ride. At its base, the Powerbite is the "elevator pitch," a concise, high-impact speech delivered between the first and fifth floors. But the real beauty of the Powerbite is its versatility as a template for persuasions of any length or purpose.

How to Build a Powerbite

The Powerbite turns the traditional scientific or legal approach to exposition and argument on its head. It starts with the conclusion, advances two or three pieces of evidence for that conclusion, and then calls the audience to action or tells them what it means to them – all in concise, forceful, vivid language.

The basic recipe for building a Powerbite:

Begin by asserting your "conclusion." Try to limit this statement to one compelling sentence.

Next, present the evidence for your assertion. You can use facts, data points, or anecdotal stories, but don't use more than three pieces of evidence.

Finish by calling your audience to action or by telling them what it all means to them. This is the payoff, the answer to your listeners' unspoken "So what ... Why should I care?"

Examples of Powerbites

Here are a few Powerbites to help you get started.

✔

The 20-second
Powerbite

A sell-myself Powerbite (similar to the elevator speech)

I answer the question "What do you do?"

Conclusion	"I help people tell their stories."
Evidence	"Through strategic messaging and media training, I help CEOs successfully engage and persuade important audiences."
Evidence	"Through presentation development, I assist healthcare leaders as they use compelling communication to transform care."
Evidence	"Through persuasive storytelling, I help lawyers win in the courtroom."
So what?	"Got an important story to tell? I can help."

A longer version with more details

Conclusion	"I help people make high-stakes, highly successful persuasions in their own particular style."
Evidence	"I help leaders at technology companies like Microsoft, Dolby, and LinkedIn generate compelling thought leadership, launch new products and successfully engage key audiences."
Evidence	"I help healthcare leaders at The Cleveland Clinic, Kaiser Permanente, and Tenet Healthcare drive quality, efficiency and customer service improvement through leadership communications excellence."
Evidence	"I help lawyers at firms like Fenwick and West, Sidley Austin and Liebert Cassidy pitch their practices, better prepare witnesses, and win with storytelling in the courtroom."
So what?	"I can help you accelerate your success with transformed communication, presentation and persuasion skills."

A Powerbite to persuade

Here is an example of a Powerbite to persuade you that Egencia is the best choice for your corporate travel needs.

The Powerbite template is the perfect persuasion tool.

Conclusion	"Egencia delivers efficiency and cost savings that go straight to your bottom line while helping you satisfy your employee travel needs."
Evidence	"Our services to you and your employees are broad and comprehensive: attentive account management, mobile solutions, and proprietary technologies to manage the details of your travel, from booking to expense reimbursement."
Evidence	"Our Supply Chain boasts more than 130,000 negotiated hotel partners, in addition to extensive air/car partnerships, leveraging both Expedia's buying power and Egencia's expertise in the corporate market to deliver savings and added value services."
Evidence	"Like many of our customers, The Dannon Company lowered its agency fees by fifty percent; and even managed to reduce average air ticket prices by five percent despite rising airfares year over year … all while satisfying its employees."
So what?	"When it is time to review your existing travel program, Egencia will add value to your process and prove a beneficial business partner to you and your company."

Now, let's take a deeper look at the components of a successful Powerbite.

Conclusion – Your Opening Assertion

It's no simple task to start with your conclusion. As rational, logical beings, we're used to working up to a conclusion – we find it by thinking through the entire message. For this reason, it may take a good bit of time and effort to formulate your conclusion. And for the same reason, it's always a good idea to go back and revise and sharpen your opening assertion after you've finished drafting the complete Powerbite.

Evidence – Apply the Rule of Three.

Why a maximum of three pieces of evidence? As any experienced salesman will tell you, never sell beyond the close – all you do is risk losing the sale. There's no

Three is the
magic number.

point piling on the proof, hoping to persuade your audience with the sheer weight of it, when all it will really do is confuse them.

How elaborate – and lengthy – should your evidence be? That depends on where, when, and how you're using a Powerbite. For example, when using a Powerbite as the proverbial elevator pitch or as the answer to a question, conciseness counts; it's best to keep your evidence short and sweet. When you "have the floor" for a longer time or you face an openly skeptical audience, you're justified in presenting a more elaborate, detailed set of proof points.

"So What" – The Call to Action

ABC – Always be closing. Tell them what they should do based upon the compelling evidence. Tell them what all of this compelling evidence means to them personally. Ideally, the payoff should be more personal in nature than the initial assertion. Remember, it's primarily about your audience – not you, your product, or your strategy. But the payoff should also be direct and concise.

One of its functions is to restate the conclusion in different words while wrapping up your Powerbite. Another function, if I may put it more bluntly, is to get you to stop talking.

More Examples of Compelling Powerbites

Notice the next two Powerbites are only partially scripted. The speakers know their top line messages but will rely on the needs of the moment to determine which stories to tell, descriptions to provide or data to bring forth.

A physician leader recruits a promising specialist:

Conclusion	"You will be working with a healthcare leader in a satisfying and sustainable practice, fueled by the best in medical technologies."
Evidence	"We are the quality leader. In this era of transparency our leading quality metrics differentiate us from the competition." (Insert data zingers.)
Evidence	"Our personalized care commitment creates an exceptional work environment for patients, physicians and healthcare professionals." (Tell the heartfelt workplace story.)
Evidence	"Our centers of excellence, integrated care model, and automated medical records give you the leading edge tools to provide the best care for your patients." (Share examples.)

So what? "We offer you a satisfying and sustainable medical practice with a healthcare leader that stands as the model for American healthcare."

A legal firm speaks to potential clients:

Conclusion "Liebert Cassidy is the only place to turn for your labor and employment counsel."

Evidence "Our team approach puts world-class experience on your side, whatever the issue." (Insert selective bios of partners or "walk down the hall" story of collaboration.)

Evidence "Our aggressive prevention education will lower your risk of litigation." (Describe legal education workshops.)

Evidence "If you do need to take an issue to court, we have the experience and know-how to provide the best advocacy." (Provide data, a client testimonial or a compelling case study.)

So what? "Expert legal counsel could make the crucial difference in your company's success and/or your career. Bar none – Liebert Cassidy is your best choice going forward."

An executive promotes a strategy change:

Context: In our business, 80% of our key engagements are one-on-one and on the move – hallways, conference rooms, work spaces, break rooms, taxis and the hotel lobby. Digital devices and apps are all the rage. Everyone loves them. No one in our competitive space has rolled out a thoughtful and sustainable strategy for using digital storytelling to differentiate their products.

Conclusion Given where and how we need to engage our potential customers, our rapid development and deployment of interactive digital selling tools will accelerate our success with potential customers and differentiate us from the competition.

Evidence App-based digital selling tools shared on iPad and tablet devices tell a much more compelling story to our potential customers. (Demo BETA of new app.)

Evidence App-based selling tools can be continually updated and improved based on effectiveness measurement. Apps are also more cost effective than the old-school

The Powerbite is an effective way to drive change.

	printed brochures, which are out of date the day they are printed. (Use outdated brochure as prop.)
Evidence	Early evidence shows that potential customers spend more time with our associates when a digital tool is in use – especially when we hand the device over to the customer. (Share anecdote.)
So what?	We must immediately double our investment in an industry-leading digital selling strategy and accelerate its implementation.

How to Use Powerbites

The Powerbite is the backbone for any type of persuasion.

Powerbites are extraordinarily versatile. You can use them in all kinds of ways and contexts and for all kinds of purposes. That's why I urge virtually all my clients to develop a set of Powerbites for all their important communications challenges.

To "Hook"

A Powerbite can function as your "hook" for a visitor to your place of business or tradeshow booth. It can serve as a way of introducing yourself to someone you meet at a conference or a cocktail party.

To Set the Stage for a Longer Conversation

As your contributions to a conference or panel discussion, Powerbites will help audience members quickly grasp and long remember your message. Along with the moderator and your fellow speakers, the audience will also appreciate your brevity, in contrast to the windbag who hogs the microphone without saying anything of substance.

To Serve as Meeting Strategy

One CEO I know takes Powerbites into meetings as the secret weapon of his persuasion. He knows what he wants his audience to conclude. He knows which three compelling pieces of evidence to use. He knows his call to action. But he does not know how, in what order, or in how much detail he will use the arrows in his quiver.

To Power an Entire Speech or PowerPoint Presentation

A single Powerbite can become the blueprint for an entire speech. As components of a speech, Powerbites can serve as a direct, dramatic opening; as an evidence roadmap and as a "to-summarize-so-far" signpost in the body of the speech; and as a high-impact, memorable conclusion. I have built many a PowerPoint deck with the first slide as the conclusion, the next nine slides supporting three pieces of evidence and a final slide concluding or calling to action.

To Answer Common Questions

I believe that Powerbites are the most effective way of answering questions. Most of us are asked the same questions over and over in our professional lives (and our personal lives, too, I suppose). What do you do? Why should I buy your product? Why are we making this change? Is this the best strategy? Powerbites can simplify your life by providing answers to such recurring questions without having to compose a new response each time. They can also help you give your best answer every time – one that you've drafted, reduced and rehearsed for maximum impact.

To Use for Any Communication Challenge

One of the greatest gifts you can give yourself as a communicator is a supply of carefully crafted Powerbites for each communications challenge you face: product launches, management and employee meetings, strategic and organizational initiatives, press conferences, analyst briefings, performance reviews, career changes, you name it.

You can swap out pieces of evidence to suit the audience.

Dressing Up Your Powerbites

In Powerbites, every word counts, and the richer, more vivid, more specific the language you use, the more impact your Powerbites will have. More than one executive has let the air out of a presentation by using the word "amazing" over and over. I've compiled the following list of adjectives that can be substituted for that tired old term. I recommend that you compile your own list of forceful, energetic words to punch up your Powerbites.

unique	electric	inspired
matchless	exciting	immense
extraordinary	confident	vast
rare	jazzed	infinite
distinctive	stoked	ingenious
one-of-a-kind	energized	creative
singular	hopeful	huge

Dynamic language powers the Powerbite.

incomparable	eager	original
exceptional	thrilled	limitless
astonishing	powerful	eye-popping
remarkable	intense	rich
startling	deep	far-reaching
surprising	extreme	astounding
mind-blowing	dynamic	gripping
passionate	dazzling	brilliant
jaw-dropping	potent	breathtaking
fun	competitive	majestic

Cascading Powerbites

Powerbites are compelling proofs spiced by rich evidence. Yet very often a single piece of evidence can serve as the conclusion for a new Powerbite. In this way, the Powerbite will cascade and lead to new levels of persuasion.

Take for example the effort to differentiate the Xbox 360 and Kinect. The "umbrella" Powerbite for 360 will celebrate blockbuster games, the Xbox Live service and the revolutionary Kinect for Xbox 360. But Blockbuster Games, Xbox Live and Kinect are also stand-alone stories worth telling with a Powerbite. By cascading your Powerbites, you create a more robust architecture for your many persuasions.

Let's start with this Powerbite.

Conclusion	"Xbox 360 is transforming entertainment in your living room."
Evidence	"With exclusive titles like Halo, Gears of War, Fable, and Forza Motorsport plus a better experience with Call of Duty, Battlefield and The Elder Scrolls Skyrim, Xbox 360 is the home for immersive blockbuster games."
Evidence	"Xbox Live – the largest social entertainment network in the living room – gives you all your entertainment with the people you care about; games, movies, live TV, video, music, news and sports."
Evidence	"Kinect makes technology invisible. With Kinect, 'You are the Controller.' Kinect revolutionizes not only game play but the way you find and enjoy your entertainment."

So what?	"Jump in to Xbox 360 and Kinect! All the entertainment you want with the people you care about made easy!"

In the full Powerbite, I am focused on selling Xbox 360 with Kinect. But you can see that we could cascade new Powerbites from each of those three pieces of evidence. For instance, my first cascade provides detailed proof that Xbox is the home for the best blockbuster games. Here's how:

Create a new Powerbite from one piece of evidence:

Conclusion	"Xbox 360 is the best place to find and play Blockbuster Games."
Evidence	A deep dive into describing exclusive titles, their popularity and what makes them so fun
Evidence	Detailed descriptions of Xbox Live exclusive communities where all the best gamers, best competition and most fun are happening
Evidence	A compelling description of the superior industrial design featuring the sleeker look, quieter operation and Wi-Fi capability
So what?	"If you care about the best and most immersive games, Xbox 360 is the platform for you."

Powerbites can build on each other to create new persuasions.

Powerbites Come in Different Sizes.

As I've noted when discussing the use of evidence, in some contexts you'll make a Powerbite most powerful by making it brief. In other contexts, you can give a Powerbite more scope. You can enrich the language, use more detail, and relate longer anecdotes as evidence. (In the next chapter, "Storytelling," I address the importance of stories in persuasive communications.) I recommend that you create both short and long versions of your Powerbites to use as the occasion demands.

Change tone, emphasis and language for each audience.

Remember that every act of communication must be tailored for the audience. In a legal firm, for example, a Powerbite designed for potential clients will require some modification before you can use it with a recruit or a new hire. In healthcare, you might use the same basic Powerbites to deliver key messages to patients, vendors, and regulators – but because those different audiences "speak different languages," you'd want to recast your Powerbites for each one. Powerbites built for a product launch can be used to address customers, the channel, the analyst community, and others – but you'll need to adjust the language, tone, and emphasis for each group.

So as you develop your arsenal of Powerbites, make sure you create variations that are appropriate for the many audiences you'll face.

Consider, for example, how differing audiences can impact the So what? or call to action of a Powerbite.

✔

Tweak a single Powerbite and tailor the same message to each unique audience.

Our Xbox 360 Powerbite with audience-specific "So what?"

Audience	So what?
Consumers (Original)	"Jump into Xbox 360! All your entertainment with the people you care about made easy."
Retail Partners	"Xbox 360 will be #1 in driving your console, software and accessories attach rates this holiday."
Industry Analysts	"Xbox 360 is the innovation leader with a competitive advantage that comes from bringing together great games and entertainment, social networks and ease of use."
Financial Analysts	"Xbox 360 will be the best-selling console worldwide in the year ahead, while Kinect and Xbox Live have changed the financial tail of this console generation."
Technology Analysts	"The Xbox 360 platform confirms that innovative hardware, premium content, and great UX supported by the cloud will drive the future of premium digital entertainment."

So What? Powerbites Work.

As a communications professional, I offer a wide range of strategies to suit all sorts of situations and personalities. But at the end of the day, it's the Powerbite that stands out as a universally appreciated tool.

Clients of all types express their new-found love of Powerbites with comments similar to these:

> "The Powerbite anchored my persuasion in this career-defining meeting."

> "What a great forcing function. Whenever I'm addressing a tough issue, I approach it by building my Powerbite."

> "Finally I have a simple and easy answer to the once difficult question – "What do you do?""

> "When people come into my office and starting rambling, I tell them to stop – regroup and return with a Powerbite."

> "This is like saying what you are going to say, saying it again, and then saying what you've said. Now I have to discipline myself to use it more often."

> "I actually keep Powerbites in my hip pocket. It keeps me from feeling as if I am building my answers on the fly."

> "Powerbites have made my team more compelling and disciplined – could you please teach the tool to our leader!"

The power of persuasion is about being prepared. With Powerbites, you are.

Powerbites impact your way of working.

Exercise: Building a Powerbite

Powerbite Practice

Create two Powerbites to answer the question, "What do you do?

First, compose a 90-second version. Then reduce the sauce to craft a version you can deliver in 20 or 30 seconds.

The Powerbite Template:

Conclusion

Evidence

Evidence

Evidence

So what?

Chapter 6

Storytelling

Great Storytellers are Great Persuaders.

We need story; otherwise the tremendous randomness of experience overwhelms us. Story is what penetrates. – Robert Coover, Brown University

Stories are powerful tools for persuasion.

The need for story runs deep in our species. Cultures define themselves through stories called myths. Religions embody their values and beliefs in stories. Nations rely on stories – the Trojan War, the six wives of Henry the Eighth, the Great Depression – to conceptualize, understand, and pass down their histories from generation to generation. Parents tell stories to teach their children. Stories are what we use to try to make sense of the world and ourselves. As the philosopher Kenneth Burke said, "Stories are equipment for living."

We learn to talk and listen by having people read stories to us, and we learn to read by parsing their words and sentences for ourselves. Story is the very essence of our narrative and dramatic arts, from epic poetry and the novel to theater, film, and television. Even the news of the day is packaged in the form of stories. Why are stories so powerful, so important, so central to our lives?

Stories help us compare notes about being human.

To begin with, stories are mostly about people. We are a gossipy tribe. From the back fence to Broadway, the campfire to the Facebook page, we never tire of telling and hearing stories, about ourselves and about others. Stories give us a way to compare notes about being human. Stories present us with actions we have done or can imagine doing, experiences we have had or can imagine having.

Stories are about feelings.

In contrast to the proofs of logic or appeals to reason, which speak to the brain, stories speak to the heart. Stories go to our core.

Stories are dramatic.

Whether played out by actors, read from the page, shared around a kitchen or conference room table, or told from a podium, great stories command our attention with that irresistible question: What will happen next? They can draw us to the edge of our seats – literally – in anticipation of the answer, and they can take our breath away when they deliver it.

Stories are persuasive.

Finally, and most important in the context of this book, stories are persuasive. Don't get me wrong. Stories told purely to entertain have value, and I've watched many speakers use such stories to make themselves and the occasion memorable, which can only enhance the impact of a presentation.

Stories make the point.

That said, the great power and purpose of stories in business and professional communications is to make a point. You can claim that your product or service is superior; but you can prove it with a story. You can spell out your company's principles or cultural values; but you can illustrate and validate them with stories. You can describe what "differentiates" your brand; but you can make your brand both unmistakable and unforgettable with stories. You can suggest that people act or change, or even ask them directly; but with a well-told story, you can jolt them into action.

Which type of story sends your message most effectively?

Storytelling Types and Examples

In my experience, six types of stories are most common – and, I believe, most effective – in business and professional presentations:

- The Anecdote

- The Powerbite Story

- The Cautionary Tale

- The Hero Story

- The Aspirational Story

- The Analogy

Of course, many stories are a combination of two or more of these types. But let's consider the six basic types before turning our attention to the techniques of effective storytelling.

The Anecdote

The Greek root of the word anecdote means "unpublished items," and indeed anecdotes are usually just that: brief narratives of events that never made the six o'clock news or the *New York Times*. People sometimes speak of "anecdotal evidence" dubiously, if not with scorn. But in a presentation, anecdotes can often serve to prove a point more effectively than a dry set of facts. Here are several examples:

A leader's anecdote highlights her team's obstacle to growth.

> As part of my onboarding process, I sat down and read through the 360-degree reviews of my current leadership team. In scouring those fifty documents from cover to cover – yes, it was a major investment of time – I found exactly one suggestion for performance or behavior improvement. One! My team is either perfect, clueless, or lacking the trust to pursue excellence together.

In this sales pitch, an anecdote differentiates the technology.

> Listen to this email from one of our clients: "A number of our employees were stranded in Europe recently due to the volcanic activity in Iceland. Without your booking tool, I think many of them might still be stuck! But what I really appreciate is that your technology provided visibility. I was able to relay accurate details about individual employee's whereabouts to more than one panicked loved one."

Here's a "Don't Wait – Communicate" anecdote.

> The other day just before surgery, Mary called a time-out. Something wasn't right. There had been a complication in the previous surgery. It was successfully resolved, but the buzz was still in the air. A team member said something about rushing to catch up. The surgeon was on the phone during the transition and entered the operating room at the last minute. Thank goodness Mary acted on her instinct and called the time-out. The team was about to commence on a wrong-site surgery. Mary is new to the team but living proof that in our organization, everyone is empowered to act for patient safety.

This anecdote encourages efficient work habits and collaboration.

> Last week our newest associate, Pauline, faced an issue that was new to her. Rather than reinventing the wheel, racking up billable hours and angering our client, she shrewdly put out a call for team members who have already navigated this FLSA issue. Leveraging our collective expertise like this means she not only saved our client hours of expense, but she also provided a better answer faster.

Infuse your presentation with bite-size anecdotes.

A simple anecdotal tale proves a point.

A longer anecdote makes a point about patient communication:

Dr. Avila recently experienced a moment all doctors fear. He made a medical error during a routine colonoscopy. Thank goodness the error was detected early, and a potentially life-threatening infection was avoided. But in the meantime, the patient and her husband were extremely anxious and very angry.

There was no question that a mistake had been made, and a lawsuit was a very real possibility. In the past, Dr. Avila would have avoided further contact with the patient and her family, lest anything he might say would further expose his liability. But he had recently completed our training program in risk management, where he learned that a provider can express concern and sorrow in such a situation – that, in fact, he should express concern and sorrow – without incurring greater liability.

As a result, Dr. Avila was able to sit down with the patient and her husband to express his sincere regret over the event. He explained what had happened during the procedure, then talked about steps he was already taking to make sure that such an error would not happen again. Human and heartfelt, his honesty served as a first step in mending the provider-patient relationship and, ultimately, helped us avoid a costly lawsuit. During their exit briefing, the patient and her husband expressed their appreciation for Dr. Avila and stated that, from their point of view, the case was closed.

This is just one example of how honest, whole-hearted communication with patients can reduce our exposure to lawsuits. Now let me show you some statistics that prove how the training and skills Dr. Avila brought to bear on his case are having a positive impact on risk across our organization.

Notice how the speaker first told a story to dramatize and humanize the issues, then turned to the statistics showing that risk management training benefits everyone in the organization, not just the individual featured in the story. This is the power of the anecdote, to engage an audience in a particular case as a means of driving home a broader point.

Anecdote in a fundraising speech for a religious studies consortium

The day after Christmas last year, we learned that an earthquake-triggered tsunami had struck coastal areas surrounding the Indian Ocean.

It was a faraway disaster – literally on the other side of the world – and at first our media tried to "bring it home" to us with stories of Western tourists who were there, caught in the wrong place at the wrong time.

But as the death toll mounted, it became clear that the story was not about Western tourists. On the western-most Indonesian island of

Sumatra, which was closest to the epicenter and already in turmoil because of civil war, more than 100,000 people had died. Half a million were left homeless.

And in villages along the coast, the tsunami had also destroyed the fishing industry, which the people there depend on for food, for trade, for life itself.

A death toll over 150,000, and a human toll that staggered the imagination – that's what brought the story home to concerned people everywhere.

One such person – a man I know because he happens to be one of our donors – felt called upon to do something in the wake of that faraway disaster. He wanted to help restore the fisheries in the coastal villages of Sumatra. So he offered a million dollars to put the boats back in the water. And the aid organization he offered the money to – they turned him down.

Because, you see, he's Jewish – and the tsunami victims of Sumatra were mostly Muslims.

Isn't that typical of the world today? Just one more irony in our sad, ironic times?

I hope not. I hope we're still capable of understanding such episodes as tragic – all the more so because we've come to think of them as typical.

Notice how the greater part of the story was given over to exposition; the Indian Ocean tsunami of late 2004 is what set up the drama of the story – what was at stake – so the speaker took his time establishing and letting the audience connect with that background. Then, at the end, the speaker drove home the point of the anecdote in a distinctive way: first he offered himself and the audience a chance to distance themselves from the outcome as "just one more irony," and then he forcefully withdrew that option.

The Powerbite Story

Simply put, this is a series of anecdotes strung together as the evidence in a Powerbite. Instead of data, facts, or assertions, you use an exemplary or illustrative anecdote for each piece of evidence.

The Powerbite

For example, here's a Powerbite about a legal firm that specializes in labor and employment issues (used as an example in Chapter 5):

Use a Powerbite story to persuade.

Conclusion	LCW is the only place to turn for your labor and employment counsel.
Evidence	Our aggressive preventative education will lower your risk of litigation.
Evidence	Our team approach puts world-class experience at your command.
Evidence	If you do need to take an issue to court, we have the experience and know-how to provide you with the best advocacy.
So what?	Because expert legal counsel could make the difference in your company's success and your career, LCW is your best choice.

The Powerbite turned into a story.

And here's a "translation" of that Powerbite into the story of a city manager whose career is enhanced by use of effective counsel:

Look for the structure of the Powerbite in this story.

"Phillip Gets Promoted"

A Valentine City administrator named Phillip Whitman is just one of the many clients we serve here at LCW. He's been attending our workshops in conflict resolution, discipline, evaluations, and more for the last six years, and as he'll be the first to tell you, that training has helped him in countless ways.

For example, he's developed a "don't wait" approach to employee feedback and performance evaluation. Not only did this help him justify the reassigning of an under-performing staff member, it also improved overall morale among his team.

But Phillip's most compelling success at the city involved the restructuring of his department to better serve the community. At one point, three of our partners joined forces to help him navigate the most complex aspects of the personnel changes. Phillip loves to tell the story of the conference call he had with two additional partners, during which one rattled off legal requirements while the other offered tips and learnings from a similar process we had just completed with another client.

In court, we were pleased to represent Phillip and the city and prevail in a case that helped set a precedent for cities trying to improve their services to the community.

And we are proud to say that Phillip Whitman has recently been promoted by the city of Valentine – a promotion he richly deserves.

Notice how the story follows the structure of the Powerbite, with an incident or detail serving to document each piece of evidence and to answer the question, "So what?"

The Cautionary Tale

"Train wrecks" are irresistible spectacles. Who doesn't like a woeful tale of failure, heartbreak, or horror? The patient who got "backwatered" in the emergency room and nearly died. The potentially ruinous liability lawsuit brought about by a perfect storm of product failure and organizational dysfunction. The price that had to be paid when a company went too long without paying attention to customers.

Here's one such story an executive used in a presentation to the employees of his company.

> "Failure to Implement"
>
> Last quarter our sales team sold applications to fifty new customers, and we promised they'd be up and running within three months. But because they had bought multiple applications, these customers started getting calls from several of our implementation teams, who all asked them the same questions and asked them to fill out the same forms.
>
> Naturally, the customers started to complain. But our sales team didn't get the head's-up, and they had no way of knowing that their sweet success of the recent past was quickly turning sour.
>
> That wasn't all. As you know, our products are not integrated, the interface for each is different, and so users need different training for each application. Apparently, our training teams don't communicate with one another any better than our implementation and sales teams. So we had two or three trainers calling customers and clamoring to train them – at the same time.
>
> Is it any wonder that our fail-to-start rate with these customers is at 68 percent?

This example illustrates both the power and the perils of the cautionary tale. There can be no question what the moral of this story is – that rhetorical question at the end is like a twist of the knife. But what a downer!

Words of warning about cautionary tales

The cautionary tale is overused these days. Seduced by the doomsday drama of it all, too many speakers are opting for what's called a "burning platform" presentation, presumably in an effort to jolt the audience into action. Some of these presentations feature a tale of abject failure like the one above. In others, a single slide showing an unsustainable trend does the job of painting a

Cautionary tales move us to get off our duffs and take action!

bleak picture. But unbeknownst to these speakers of doom and gloom, many are delivering the fifth "burning platform" presentation the audience has had to endure in the last week.

Bad enough that you come off sounding like Chicken Little ("The sky is falling!"); you definitely don't want to be one of many such downcast, panicky creatures.

You may risk alienating your audience. Second, when you tell a cautionary tale, you are taking a risk: that a feeling of being blamed (and fearing the consequences) might overwhelm your audience, or that failure will be the only thing they'll remember from your presentation.

Dishearten an audience too much and you can alienate them and never get them back; they will literally tune you out for the rest of your presentation.

Balance cautionary tales with positive stories.

So I advise caution when using cautionary tales. In any case, avoid starting a presentation with a cautionary tale – that is, before you've had a chance to establish rapport and trust with the audience. And always balance a cautionary tale with something positive and upbeat: a "what we learned" plan for saving the day or doing better next time, a tale of turning the tide, a happy ending or aspirational story that restores the audience's sense of hope.

Use the hero story to inspire.

The Hero Story

Heroes are people who make a difference, which makes heroes very useful as the subject of a presentation told to make a difference. But what makes heroes heroic – and what makes their stories dramatic and compelling – is that they must overcome obstacles in order to succeed. Joan of Arc started out as the daughter of peasants, not as a priest or courtier or soldier; Horatio Alger was decidedly not born with a silver spoon in his mouth; Luke Skywalker didn't know that he could be a Jedi knight.

The scholar of mythology, Joseph Campbell, taught us to think of the hero's struggle as a journey, whether real or metaphorical. This can serve as a useful guideline when you're creating your own hero stories. Think of yourself as narrating a journey. Where does your hero set out from? What obstacles arise along the way, and how is each one overcome? What is the decisive moment in the story, sometimes called the moment of resolution, when the hero overcomes the last obstacle, arrives at his or her destination, learns or understands something new, or makes a crucial decision? In short, what happens to change the hero, or when the hero changes the world?

This story, used in the fundraising speech for the religious studies consortium, makes powerful, dramatic use of the decisive moment in the hero's journey:

> Remarkable people find their way to us in surprising ways. And they
> arrive with a sense of mission that's rooted in their faith but energized

by their experience in the world. It's their passion, their engagement, which makes the GTU a place where religion meets the world.

One of my favorite examples is Elizabeth Drescher, a doctoral student in Christian spirituality. Before coming to the GTU, Elizabeth worked for some years in health insurance. During that time, she discovered what she believed to be improper procedures that had defrauded the government and denied benefits to thousands of people. Convinced that her employer had no intention of correcting the problem, she reported it to the government.

But it's one thing to become a whistleblower, quite another to undertake doctoral studies in theology at the GTU. What brought Elizabeth to us? Here are her own words on the connection:

"My work at the GTU is aimed at understanding why people do or do not feel empowered to act upon their religious commitments. For instance, what moved in the soul of the woman who put a pile of Medicare reports on my chair with a note saying, 'I have been trying for years to get this fixed, but have been told that I'd be fired if I brought it up again. I have two small children and cannot lose my job. I've heard that you're working on this … I hope this will help you.' And, she added, 'I am praying for you.'"

It probably won't surprise you that Elizabeth's doctoral research is focused on what she calls "the faith lives of ordinary Christians."

Or that she is passionate about the connection between her research and current issues, like the role of religion in contemporary American politics.

Use the hero story to communicate core values.

It's not surprising that this story was at the heart of a speech about the values and mission of an organization. It's also interesting that it was, in fact, a story within a story: a tale of one person with certain values inspiring another, and that person in turn embodying those values for someone else (in this case, for the speaker as well as for the audience). Hero stories are especially good for communicating the core values of an organization and propagating those values through the organization and beyond.

A little less poetic, perhaps, but equally effective is the hero story in which a product, service, or system, rather than a person, is the hero. For example:

Dr. David Lawrence opened a speech before the National Press Club with the story of a 15-year-old asthma sufferer named Maria and her family. A mesmerizing storyteller, Dr. Lawrence described the trials and tribulations they endured to get Maria the care she needed in a fee-for-service medical system: the trips to the emergency room, the "near misses" when inappropriate medications were almost administered, even the disappointment of Maria's little brother that family vacation trips were out of the question because his sister could not stray from the one medical center the family could visit.

Enter the hero, as Maria and her family transition to team-based care provided by an integrated healthcare organization. The whole story changes, as the team teaches Maria and her parents better methods for controlling and treating her asthma. Her electronic medical record, including all of her prescriptions, is available to providers anywhere in the state. At the end we see the family – and a happy little brother – going on their first vacation in years because Maria's health is improved and she can count on exceptional care along the entire route.

✔

Technology can be the star of a hero story.

Though it featured a non-human hero – integrated, team-based healthcare – Dr. Lawrence's story was nevertheless rich in human interest, action, and drama. Stories in which technology is the hero, increasingly common in our ever-more digital world, can be just as effective. For example, a client who built a successful company selling bar-coding technology to hospitals told this story:

Every year thousands of patients die due to medical errors in the administration of prescriptions. And no wonder! Consider Mrs. Crosby, a woman in her seventies who arrived at the hospital for surgery with seven bottles of prescription drugs in a paper bag.

Now, the effects of her surgery had left her even less clear than she already was about which of those to take and when. The nurse on duty was overworked and tired, and the physician who prescribed Mrs. Crosby's additional post-op meds did so in his usual illegible scribble. And to top it all off, many of the medication containers, old and new, look alike.

A recipe for disaster? Of course it was – until Fairmont Hospital rolled out a simple bar code system that requires staff to scan any medication before it's given to a patient. Now Mrs. Crosby's prescriptions are entered into the system when she arrives. The physician's instructions are entered, too – and accurately deciphered in the process. And no matter how tired and distracted he or she might be, no nurse will be able to administer a medication until the system confirms that it's the right medication at the right dose.

The Aspirational Story/Futurecasting

I believe that aspirational storytelling, or futurecasting, is one of the most powerful techniques available to business and professional communicators. The aspirational story actually takes place in the future, creating a picture of what that future will look and feel like.

Futurecasting transforms aspirations into inspiration.

In an aspirational story, you can describe the change, results, innovations, systems, or values you wish to bring about. That's why this form of storytelling is so useful for leaders at every level: by giving specific, detailed, compelling form to your vision, you can transform your aspirations into inspiration for those you lead as well as for your colleagues. You can motivate people to do great things.

Perhaps because it's completely "made up" – a tale of things that have not yet come to pass – the aspirational story gives full scope to the art of storytelling. You can describe a day in the life of an organization or team, a customer or a client.

You can take the audience on an experiential journey, building in moments when a new system or product is enjoyed, a task is made simpler than ever before, something perhaps not even imagined becomes something real.

Here's an example:

> A manager at Genentech stands before her team of 250 employees. She has mocked up a copy of *The Wall Street Journal* and displays it to the audience.
>
> "I'd like to read you a front-page article from *The Wall Street Journal* of May 15th, 2015, under the headline "Genentech: Delivering Cures for Patients and Investors."
>
> The article begins like this: "With the release of its latest cancer drug, biotech pioneer Genentech has proved once again the power of genetics-based drug development to help patients seeking a cure for deadly disease as well as investors looking for healthy returns."
>
> The story jumps to page four, where it's accompanied by a sidebar under this headline: "Data Delivery Accelerates Approval Process." That's right, folks: that's our organization, right here in a front-page story in the *Journal*. According to the article, we made the crucial difference in ensuring rapid FDA approval. We are credited with getting the right information to the right people on a timely basis throughout the clinical trials and approval process. Our analytics are described as, quote, second to none in the industry, unquote. And what started the journey to this triumphant day in the year 2015? It started when we met as a team on this day in 2011 and committed to three key objectives that gave us focus, drove our decisions, and inspired our excellence in the years to come.

This leader uses the aspirational story as a hook to introduce her strategic priorities. To be sure, both she and her audience know that these priorities will require hard work and change. She is counting on the aspirational story to motivate that change.

The Analogy

As the playwright Christopher Fry wrote, "What a wonderful thing is metaphor!" By using one thing to describe another, analogies actually help people see things differently and often, therefore, more clearly – in a new light, so to speak.

Paint a vivid picture of the destination and they will clamor to get on board.

Analogies can be long or short. In his book *Raising the Bar: Integrity and Passion in Life and Business*, outdoor adventurer and Clif Bar founder Gary Erickson tells a story (originally used in a presentation) of a failed climb up an icy mountain face as an analogy for a period when his company lost its focus, adaptability, and initiative. Another leader I worked with used a brief analogy we can all relate to – the panic of trying to find the windshield wipers in a rental car when a sudden downpour rendered him virtually blind at 60 miles per hour – to highlight why a common user interface is essential to the future of his industry.

Often known as a parable, the analogy has a long and honorable history in religion and myth. The following story, used by a data processing executive in his keynote address at a client conference, draws on scripture for an analogy.

Help your audience see the world in a different light.

> Let me begin with a very old story: the story of the Tower of Babel, from the Bible's Book of Genesis.
>
> As you may remember, this is a story about Noah's descendants. The first thing we're told about them – and this is very important – is that they shared a common language. The next thing we know, they settle in Babylon, and they decide to build a tower that reaches up to heaven. It's their way of making a name for themselves.
>
> But God sees this tower, and he – or she – doesn't like it one bit. Too presumptuous. If mankind succeeds with this, who knows what they'll try next, right? So God takes away their common language, and scatters them in confusion. And that puts an end to work on the tower. After all, it's tough to build a tower to heaven when you can't understand what the guy next to you is saying. I wouldn't be surprised if you've heard this story before, applied to our industry and the way we've been using technology. Building the Tower of Babel gets lost in the babble. Instead of a common language, we have the confusion and conflict of many systems and tools and applications. There's lots of talk, but not much understanding.

Notice how the speaker recast the story in modern colloquial language, making sure to avoid offending anyone's religious sensibilities while encouraging the audience to see themselves in the story. Notice, too, that the speaker was very explicit in articulating the moral of the story and relating it to the audience.

Time to Revive a "Lost Art"

Given the power of storytelling, I've been surprised to discover how rarely stories are used in today's business and professional presentations. Among my clients, I've found that lawyers are the most likely to recognize the importance of storytelling. Perhaps this is because so much of the law is case law – fundamentally a body of stories. In a certain sense, too, litigation is a form of competitive storytelling, and many of the greatest litigators in history have been superb storytellers.

But among most professionals and business people, it seems, storytelling has become a lost art. (Even litigators, I've observed, lose the knack when conducting the business and management sides of their profession.) Has storytelling fallen victim to the hurry-up pace of the workaday world? When facing audiences who demand facts and figures, logic and proof, are we afraid that they'll regard stories with suspicion – that they'll find our stories artificial, at best ambiguous, at worst frivolous? As we've become dependent on presentation software that's more about the software than the presentation, has storytelling been felled by a hail of bullet points?

Whatever the reasons we may have turned away from it, I'm a ferocious advocate for reviving the lost art of storytelling in business and professional communications. As demonstrated, I hope, by the examples I've described, stories have an unparalleled power to command attention and engage the heart as well as the mind: theirs is the true power of persuasion.

Besides, it's just plain fun to tell and listen to stories. Whether you're the speaker or an audience member, you can count on storytelling to give any presentation an extra charge of vitality.

So what keeps more people from exploiting this potent form of communication? In most cases, I've found, it's fear. You can't imagine how often I hear people marvel at the great stories they hear and the people who tell them – and then claim that they themselves are just no good at telling stories.

I don't buy it. As I started this chapter by saying, we all tell and hear stories all the time. We have a natural affinity for stories and storytelling. And we can all become good storytellers.

How to Tell a Story

Basic Story Structure

Storytelling is a narrative form, which is to say that the fundamental axis of a story is time: "This happened, then this happened, then …" Of course, a series of simply random events do not a story make; there has to be something that holds the events together in a coherent whole.

The simplest way to describe the structure of a story is that it has a beginning, a middle, and an end. Just as important, to command our attention and hold our interest, what happens in a story must happen to someone. In fact, it is that someone who holds the events together. Every story has a leading character, known in drama as the protagonist, whose actions and experiences engage the audience's interest.

As Aristotle explained in his observations on Greek drama, the most compelling stories reach a turning point in either a moment of reversal in the fortunes of the protagonist, or a moment of recognition when the protagonist learns something new, or both. In any case, the protagonist is changed.

Adding up these observations, we might describe the structure of most stories like this:

1. Something happens to someone …

2. That person and others take action in response to what has happened …

3. And the final result is that change takes place – in the external or internal circumstances of the protagonist.

Adding a little more detail, here's how I'd describe the basic building blocks for a story:

Anybody can tell a story using the basic building blocks.

"Once upon a time…"

Implicitly, at least, just about all stories begin with the classic fairy tale opening, as the storyteller introduces us to the protagonist and other characters (the subjects of the story) and the setting (when and where it takes place). This part of the story is also known as the exposition.

"Then one day…"

Something happens, and that "something" triggers the rest of the action of the story, usually propelling the protagonist on the path to some goal. In drama and screenwriting, the triggering event is often called the inciting incident.

"And then… and then… and then…"

The plot thickens, as one action or event after another unfolds. In dramatic writing, these developments are known as complications because, well, things get complicated. In well-crafted stories, each complication results from and/or builds on the one before it.

"Until at last…"

In drama, this is called the resolution or denouement – from the French word *desnouer*, "to untie" – as the story's big knot of complications gets untangled. For Aristotle, this is the so-called moment of reversal. In any case, it is the all-important moment of change.

"And the moral of the story is…"

This is the end. The cliché about "the moral of the story" is usually reserved for children's stories or, if used in stories told by and for adults, it's used somewhat ironically. But in business and professional presentations, it's important to close a story with the end results, the lessons learned, the benefits reaped ("And because of that …" or "And ever since then …"). Indeed, interpreting or elaborating on the meaning of a story, as described in the next section, can be a very persuasive tactic.

Add Descriptive Coloring.

As a reader or listener, you know there's more to storytelling than simply saying "what happened." You know that much of the power of a story comes from the art with which it is told. Here are a few basic techniques for making your stories more engaging, more dramatic, more persuasive:

Make it dramatic.

Without drama, a story is just one thing happening after another. Keeping your eye on the structure of your story can help you make it dramatic. What do you need to reveal during the exposition at the beginning to set up the plot and "seed" the tension? Just as important, what do you need to conceal? How many actions and events (complications), told in how much detail, will build the tension without exhausting the patience of the audience? At what point exactly should your denouement arrive, and what's the most effective way of delivering it?

Insert vivid details and emotive coloring to engage.

When you show an audience a PowerPoint presentation or demonstrate a product, they all see the same thing. When you tell them a story, you engage them as collaborators, inviting them to imagine the story in their own minds. That's what makes storytelling so powerful. And that's why it's essential to use language and imagery that makes your story vivid in the "mind's eye" of each listener.

Colorful language adds impact.

With descriptive coloring, you use words to paint a picture of what the characters and settings look like, to tell how people behaved and not just what they did. Such details add texture and specificity to the characters and events. With emotional coloring, you enable your audience to connect and empathize with what the characters feel.

Here are some examples of both kinds of coloring:

- He sailed into the room looking like some sort of high-tech rock star.

- Realizing that finger-pointing would be a colossal waste of time, they trudged back to their cubicles, back to square one.

- You could see the steam coming out of her ears, and you wished to be anywhere in the world but standing in front of her.

- The results jolted the industry like a hundred million volts, and back at the office we popped the corks on a case of champagne.

- The defendant sat stony-faced as the judge read the verdict to a dead-silent courtroom.

Use Multiple Points of View.

A good story becomes great when you approach it from multiple points of view.

Take, for example, the story about bar code technology and the difference it can make in a hospital. Told from the point of view of patients, the technology saves lives. Told from the point of view of the nurse, it saves her bacon. Told from the point of view of the physician, it saves a patient and protects a reputation. Told from the point of view of the hospital's risk manager, it saves the hospital from litigation. And told from the point of view of the CEO or marketing officer, it differentiates the hospital from others.

Vary the Rate and Cadence.

Good storytellers have a sense of speech as music – that is, they know how to vary the volume, pitch, and rhythm of their voices to suit each moment in the story. During the exposition, as the characters and situation are introduced, a good storyteller usually goes at a careful and measured pace. As the conflict starts to heat up and tension builds, the pace quickens. And just before the dramatic climax, there's often a "pregnant pause" as the audience waits to hear what will happen next … and the storyteller makes them wait. Then, from the climax or resolution to the end of the story, the storyteller often reverts to the relaxed pace of the exposition.

In large part, making a story sing is a matter of responding to it emotionally yourself, as you tell it. You don't have to be a great actor to do this; with some of the techniques described in Section III for using your voice and body effectively, you can make your stories sing.

Interpret your story to drive the point home.

Share the Moral of Your Story.

When the purpose of a story is persuasion, as opposed to pure entertainment, interpreting it is often necessary, and always effective, in "closing the deal." Having told the story, you circle back, analyze it, and elaborate on what it means. This is what a leader in healthcare did at the end of a hero story about a doctor saving a child's life:

> The point of this story is not that one individual did something Herculean, something no one else is likely to emulate. On the contrary, the point is that this physician's experience is not unique in our organization. We are structured so that every physician can have immediate access to a specialist – our governance puts the choice in your hands and not those of a bean-counter or utilization review board. Electronically making lab results available to both you

and a specialist, even hundreds of miles away, is standard operating procedure.

So your decision-making can always be based on all the medical evidence and the most expert consultation.

That's why I'm so proud to be part of this organization, and so confident in our ability to provide superior care.

Give Every Story a Title.

By starting off a story with a title, you can pique the audience's interest – and give them a way to remember the story later. Even if you don't share it with the audience, giving a title to every story you plan to tell will force you to think about why you're telling it. You'll focus better on the story's theme, essence, or core message – and the story will be the better for it.

Build a Story Room.

Every successful business succeeds by differentiating its products and services, their features and benefits, in the eyes of its customers. Likewise, every enterprise, institution, company, department, group, team, and partnership is built on certain core values that bind all the members together in a shared understanding, a common goal, a united effort.

But it's impossible to differentiate products or the values of your organization using only features, facts, and figures. And it usually doesn't work to simply lay claim to superiority. Saying that your product is faster, more powerful, or "better," that you have integrity, that you're customer-focused or innovative, that you care about your employees or your community – as often as not, such assertions provoke doubt or even derision. "After all," your audience is likely to think, "doesn't everybody say that?" Claims sound empty without something concrete, something the listener connects with, to back them up.

Storytelling is the answer. Brought to life in stories, the key attributes and benefits of your product or service or the core values of your organization become not only credible but vivid, specific, powerful, and memorable.

Maybe yours is simply not a storytelling organization – or so you think. I've found that if you listen, and maybe do a bit of prodding, you can hear many stories, just buzzing with life and lessons, in any organization.

> Collect stories to illustrate your claims, your values and your vision.

Stories Help Differentiate.

I frequently work with clients who are planning a product launch, press tour, or other campaign to introduce their new offerings to the marketplace. One of the most useful exercises we can go through, I've found, is to gather the team in front of a big white board and build what I call "a story room."

We begin by populating the board with all the features and benefits we can imagine. Usually, the list gets pretty long, at which point it's time to reduce the sauce. When we've pared the list to the top three to five key points, the real fun begins as we challenge each other –

> "Who can tell a customer story that validates this claim about ease of use?"

> "Describe a scenario that dramatizes what we're calling the seamless integration of these new services."

> "OK – let's combine three features in a single story and make them come to life!"

As we begin to capture our stories, we give each one a title. We tell them to each other. We challenge various team members to either adapt or personalize a particular story or compose one from their direct experience that would serve the same purposes. Soon the team has developed a comprehensive storytelling strategy based on compelling and consistent content.

Stories bring key messages to light.

To give a concrete example:

> I worked with the Xbox team at Microsoft as they were preparing a new marketing campaign for the Xbox 360 video game console. The campaign was slated to begin in the holiday selling season and continue through the following six to twelve months. The core marketing objective was to establish the Xbox 360 as an entertainment and media center for entire families, a vehicle for a wide variety of social experiences – not just a console for solitary hard core video game players.

> In support of the objective, the company was introducing lots of new products and services, including the Xbox 360 Arcade bundle – Xbox 360 console with a set of five family-oriented games, built-in, parental control, new easier-to-use controllers, movie downloads from the online Xbox Live marketplace, and more.

> It was a compelling line-up of products, features, and benefits. But in the form it had assumed – a typical message grid – it was dull and lifeless. The challenge was to transform this laundry list of "messages" about a "product" into a set of stories that would enable the press, retailers, and consumers to see a new era of digital entertainment shared by families and friends, and all centered on the Xbox 360.

> Once we went to the white board and opened the story room for business, that challenge quickly became a form of entertainment for the Microsoft team. By the end of the session, we had built two

captivating, easy-to-tell stories that embodied all the key messages about the "new" Xbox 360.

The "holiday" story started with a grandmother buying the Xbox 360 Arcade bundle for her grandchildren and their parents as a holiday gift, went on to describe the family playing the five included games together, setting up the parental controls, listening to music through the Xbox, connecting their Xbox Live Camera and having a video web chat with their cousins thousands of miles away, watching a DVD on the Xbox, then downloading another movie from the Xbox Live service to watch the next day, and so on.

The "new year" story described the same family expanding their Xbox entertainment center with a hard drive, using it for DVD "movie nights" with family and friends, listening to podcasts, and building a library of games, videos, and other media to enjoy using their Xbox 360.

Stories Communicate Core Values.

In business and the professions, your organization's core values are fundamental not only to the way you work but to the way you are seen, by your clients, customers, colleagues, and community. For example, my clients at Clif Bar, Inc. proudly operate according to five distinct and distinctive business aspirations –

Core values are the moral of the story.

- Sustaining Our Brands

- Sustaining Our Community

- Sustaining Our People

- Sustaining Our Business Community

- Sustaining Our Planet

Talk to any employee of the company and the odds are very good he or she will have a story to tell about how their work is aligned with these aspirations. That organization-wide understanding of core values and the ability to articulate them in stories is what makes them work for Clif Bar.

Core values stories are like fertilizer – unless you spread them around, they don't do much good. So let me tell a little story of my own:

Some years ago I led a workshop for a prestigious Silicon Valley law firm. This company of attorneys had grown rapidly during the technology boom of the 1990s, with numerous lateral hires and an expanding pool of young associates. But the members of the firm feared that, as an organization, they were beginning to lose their identity. They scheduled an offsite gathering to deal with the issue and asked me to facilitate one of the sessions.

My strategy, I told them, would be storytelling. A few eyebrows went up, but they signed on. So during the next week I conducted individual interviews with eight members of the firm: six senior partners, one lateral partner, and one associate. I focused on two tasks with each one. First, I asked each one to tell me stories about the firm, and together we mined the core values embedded in each story. Then, after settling on the story each one would tell at the offsite, I coached them as storytellers. We worked on structuring and telling the story for maximum effect, and on interpreting the story to highlight the core values it dramatized.

For the offsite, I gathered a collection of empty packing boxes and labeled each one, in large bold print, with one of the core values that was going to be brought to life through storytelling.

When the day came, the eight storytellers took the floor, one by one, and told their tales: about serving demanding clients, making difficult decisions, coming together in teams, going the extra mile, and more. While speaking, each one stacked the appropriate core values boxes at his or her side. At the end of each story, each one explained how the story represented those values – "And the moral of the story is ..."

During the eight stories, I could tell that the "audience" was really engaged in the experience, and at the end I was satisfied that the session had delivered good value to my client.

But then something remarkable happened. In a flurry of pure improvisation, another five members of the firm stood up and told specific, detailed, even colorful stories that highlighted some of the same core values they'd just heard about and even unearthed some more. The evaluations of the session confirmed that it had made a major impact on all participants – that storytelling had helped restore their sense of identity as an organization and would help them communicate that to others:

- "Now I know who we are."

- "This gives me such a sense of pride."

- "Thank you for reminding me why the work we do is so important."

- "This will help me so much in pitching the firm."

- "Now I own these stories and I plan to tell them."

Stories communicate what your company is about.

The Moral of the Story...

In a storytelling organization, members have a powerful set of tools for communicating what makes the business special.

The trick is to establish organized ways of unearthing and sharing stories. To kick-start the effort, it's often helpful to bring in someone to facilitate a storytelling session like the ones I've described.

But there are other ways to promote the storytelling across your organization. You might make time at regular meetings for departments or working teams to share stories of a recent challenge or milestone. You might create a storytelling space, a section in the employee newsletter, a wiki or a blog, where people are encouraged to share and comment on stories about the life and history of the organization and its offerings.

Every organization can use storytelling to discover its core values, bring them to life and put them to use.

Where do your stories live?

Exercise: Chronicle Stories.

Learn to tell
a better story
by listening
to others tell
theirs.

Listening for Stories

Over the next several weeks, listen for stories and great storytellers. Start keeping a log of stories, noting the qualities that made them powerful. Practice retelling the same story, replicating the structure, the language, the pacing ... Is your version as effective as the original?

How would you title the story you heard?

What kind of story is it (hero, cautionary etc.)?

What is the lesson or moral of the story?

How might you use the story in your persuasions?

Note aspects of the storyteller's technique worth adopting...

Does this story belong in your "Storyroom"?

Chapter 7

Preparation

Preparation is the Key to Success.

With the right attitude, a visceral connection with your mission, good listening skills, and a vision to share, you have a solid foundation for building and delivering a compelling presentation. In these next three chapters, you'll learn some reliable methods for discovering and developing your message, powerful techniques for driving your message home, and ways of structuring a presentation that will command your audience's attention from start to finish.

Consider the context of your presentation as you prepare.

Many organizations have some kind of process for preparing a presentation, even if it's just "this person writes the PowerPoints, and that person makes them look good." But when I started out as a coach and consultant, I was surprised at how few clients have any kind of disciplined method for executing the most fundamental task: figuring out what they want and need to say. Fewer still have a grasp of the rhetorical and structural tools that make messages forceful to the ear and memorable in the mind.

Set the Context: Who? When? Where?

Business and marketing people often call it situational analysis. I call it setting the context. All communications take place in a context, made up of several elements. Because these circumstances will influence how you will be heard, you must take them into account as you develop what you plan to say. Before you jump into developing content, you must understand context. Sometimes you may be able to do that by asking one big question: What is the context? More often, it's a matter of determining the context by asking and answering a series of little questions.

Who makes up your audience?

As any writer will tell you, the fundamental rule of communication is to think about your audience first, last, and always. Who are you trying to persuade?

That's not one question but many. You should try to answer all the questions you can about your potential audience – questions such as these:

- What's their status? Leaders, executives, middle managers, rank-and-file? Colleagues, customers, employees?

- How do they think and how do they learn? Are they technical people, visual people, numbers people?

- What's their point of view on the issues you plan to address?

- What do they expect to hear? What do they want to hear? What do they need to hear?

- Who are you to them, and how will that influence the way they listen to you? That is, what do they know about you? What do they think and feel about you?

When are you presenting?

By this, I don't just mean what day and time you're scheduled to speak (although the time of day can affect both your energy and your audience's attention span, which is why mornings are best for presentations). More important is the "virtual" when:

- When in the product lifecycle or sales process?

- When in the history of your relationship with the audience?

- When in your budget cycle or theirs?

- When in the history of your organization or industry?

The more *when* questions you can ask and answer, the better.

Where is the presentation taking place?

This too is less a question of physical space than "virtual" space. Will you be in hostile territory – for example, at a tradeshow or analysts' meeting where you might be regarded as a competitor, an upstart, an unknown quantity? Or in friendly territory – for example, at a client conference or developers' forum where you're known as a trusted partner or likable underdog?

Of course, the *where* of your presentation is a physical matter, too. If you know what kind of facility or room you'll be using – large or small, on a stage or not, with what kind of A/V equipment, and so forth – you have to think about how that might affect your options for presenting your message and the audience's expectations.

What is really going on here?

What is the subtext?

The last but far from the least important question you must ask about the context of your presentation: What is really going on here?

In drama and literature, this is called the subtext – what the characters really want, what they really mean or think as opposed to their words and actions.

Business, professional, and organizational life often has subtext, too, with various layers of meaning lurking beneath the surface – politics, unspoken agendas, unacknowledged fears, interpersonal dynamics and tensions, unresolved issues from past interactions, scores to settle, and so forth. Chances are, some such not-so-hidden layers of meaning surround the speech, presentation, or meeting you're planning. You absolutely must take them into account in developing your message.

Assess the Opportunities and Risks.

Problem-solving usually involves risks as well as opportunities. Most of my clients in business and professional life know this. Even so, I usually advise them to think and talk through the opportunities and risks involved in the presentation, meeting, or communication campaign they're preparing.

Think of opportunities as your North Star.

Doing so serves several purposes. By laying out what's at stake, you force yourself to define how you'll measure the success of your presentation. By describing what that success will mean, you clarify your goals. And by focusing your eyes on the prize, you sharpen your motivation.

To assess the opportunities, ask yourself:

- What are your hopes and dreams for this presentation?

- What's the upside? List the specific results and benefits you'll see if everything goes perfectly and you really knock the socks off your audience.

- What's the ideal overall outcome – for your organization, your product or project, your brand, your personal reputation?

To assess the risks, ask yourself these questions:

- If your presentation goes poorly, what's the cost?

- Where will that leave your product or initiative, your brand, your organization, your personal reputation?

What's at stake?

- What kind of "damage control" will you have to do to offset the consequences if you botch this opportunity?

- How much time and what resources will such an effort require?

Define Your Objective.

You've looked at the context from all the angles, and you've probably splashed some cold water in your face with an honest assessment of the opportunities and risks. Now you're ready to start moving toward developing your message. Start with the most basic definition of your objective.

What do you want to accomplish?

Great speeches and effective presentations drive people to action. That's why a great way to define your objective is to ask yourself what you want your audience to do when you've finished talking to them. Some examples:

- I want them to sign up to be organ donors.

- I want them to ask for a meeting so we can discuss having my law firm represent them.

- I want them to volunteer to join the next round of funding for my start-up.

- I want them to understand how our software application can change their medical practice and to ask for an onsite demo.

- I want them to acknowledge the need for this important resource and ask me for a budget proposal.

Contrast these strong objectives with a very common and passive objective: *"I want to update ..."*

Purge the word "update" from your vocabulary. Even if forced to give an update, use language like "I want to engage you in the progress of ..." or "Let me share the compelling story of ..." Update has become an invitation for people to tune you out.

Having a strong objective is essential to your success as a persuader. In fact, I'll go so far as to say that once you know what you want, you are well on your way to getting it.

You may have heard of the Stanislavski system of acting. According to this system, every character in a drama has a central desire or objective (often called the motivation) that drives him or her in each scene, as well as a "super objective" for the entire play. An actor must never set foot on the stage without knowing what his or her character wants.

Just as all human feeling and behavior is driven by desire, the authentic portrayal of feeling and behavior must be rooted in desire as well. And of course, it is each character's pursuit of his or her objective, coming into conflict with external forces – including other characters in pursuit of their objectives – that creates and energizes the drama.

A strong objective improves your persuasion.

I urge my clients to operate according to Stanislavski's principles when approaching a presentation, speech, or high-stakes meeting. By defining a clear, strong objective, you'll improve your "performance" in several ways. You'll sharpen your focus on your desire to persuade. You'll become more intent on your audience – their needs, desires, and doubts, and your need to connect with them. You'll feel the urgency of wanting them to do whatever it is you want them to do, and you'll communicate that urgency.

Anticipate Obstacles.

The Stanislavski system, with its emphasis on motivation and conflict, carries over into the next crucial step in the message discovery process. Like an actor preparing to play a character in a drama, you have defined your objective. You know what you want. Now you must look ahead to the conflict. You must ask yourself what, and who, is in your way.

In my experience, most of the obstacles you can anticipate exist, so to speak, in the minds of your audience. What will they question, doubt, disagree with, or reject – and why? Pay attention to the type of each such obstacle – its character, if you will – because different kinds of obstacles demand different approaches to overcoming them.

In the listening chapter, you learned to recognize a number of obstacles to your persuasion. Use these strategies as you prepare.

Will you face obstacles of understanding?

These are the easiest to overcome, provided you take the time (which means having the patience) to educate your audience by explaining what they may not know or don't understand.

Will fear get in the way?

Will fears – of risk, change, the unknown – keep your audience from hearing, believing, or accepting what you say? Fear is a formidable adversary, especially when it's hidden, as it often is; how will you bring it out into the light and overcome it?

Will you need to light a fire?

Is there a lack of urgency in the air? Do people generally agree with you but only if you don't ask them to take action – to change – now?

Do you need to change beliefs to make the sale?

Are you going up against prejudice, bias, entitlement or a competitor's campaign of misinformation? In other words, does your audience harbor ideas or beliefs –

Build persuasions that address the obstacles head on.

whether fair or unfair – that you'll have to rebut, disprove, or dislodge before you can "sell" your ideas or proposals?

Are you presenting to an audience exhausted by the pace of change?

Have you taken inventory to determine whether your audience has enough energy to take on the next great adventure? Are they coming off an exhilarating success or an exhausting slog?

✔

Answer those tough questions with the mantra in mind.

Anticipate Tough Questions.

An excellent technique for identifying obstacles is to anticipate tough questions your audience might ask. In Chapter 12, "Winning Q&A," I discuss techniques for dealing with difficult questions (and difficult questioners). But it's never too early to consider the toughest questions you're likely to hear after you've finished your presentation. In fact, the message development process is an ideal time to start.

By anticipating the tough questions at an early stage, you can often build the answers into the body of your presentation. List five questions you'd rather not have to answer; I promise that you'll see five issues you will have to address sooner or later, and it should probably be sooner.

Find the Theme... and Apply Your Mantra.

At this stage, the obstacles to achieving your objective are not your enemies. They are your allies. They are the key to discovering what you want and need to say when you "take the stage."

By identifying obstacles and anticipating tough questions, you have broken down your objective into a set of tasks for your presentation. Now, your challenge is to turn every "Why?" or "What do you mean?" into an "I understand"... every unspoken "I'm afraid" into an outspoken "That's worth the effort or risk"... every uninformed or misinformed or timid "No" into a committed, heart-felt "Yes." In other words, each obstacle defines a key message for your presentation.

To illustrate the process of going from objective to obstacles to key messages, here I offer two examples from my experience.

A leader plans a high-stakes strategy session with her management team.

> I worked with the leader of a health food company as she prepared for a strategic planning session with the company's senior management team. Better than anyone, she knew this would be a crucial moment for the company. She also knew that the session, which she was to open with a presentation, would be a crucial moment – a career-changing moment, one way or the other – for her.

The situation was this: The company's early success was based on consistently high levels of satisfaction among retail customers: people simply loved the company's products. But success and rapid growth had undermined some crucial quality control measures and diluted customer service efforts, and customer satisfaction levels were eroding. Meanwhile, the company faced ferocious new competition from larger, long-term players in the foodstuffs industry.

My client had a plan for the company, involving some drastic changes in its infrastructure, focus, and culture. She had a plan for the company, but that didn't mean she had a plan for her presentation. She knew she'd have to do much more than simply describe her proposals and leave the room.

I suggested that she start by defining her objective, focusing on the audience. This is what she came up with:

> I want them to pledge "bet your career" support for a new company strategy focused on customer service and based on a culture of "disciplined entrepreneurship."

This objective had multiple levels, and it left some important ideas undeveloped, but that was OK. It defined what she wanted her audience to do in no uncertain terms.

Next, we worked together on anticipating the obstacles. For her, this was a matter of listing the reasons her management team might resist the plan or withhold the complete commitment that she wanted from every one of them. Here's what she came up with:

Define the objectives and then anticipate obstacles.

- Most of them don't appreciate how much our customer satisfaction levels have eroded or how much that erosion has cost us in market share and reputation.

- They probably don't realize how rapidly market conditions are changing, and they may not appreciate the threat posed by our competitors.

- They're not familiar with available customer service software solutions designed to address the problems we have.

- They can be expected to feel threatened by the idea of retraining around new software.

- They can be expected to feel even more threatened by a new, companywide emphasis on measuring customer satisfaction and rewarding ourselves and employees according to success in that area.

The first three were obstacles of understanding, and the last two combined a fear of change and an inadequate understanding of the

Answering those tough questions tells them what's in it for them!

rationale for it. Based on her list of obstacles, my client was ready to create a list of key messages – the ideas she knew she would have to explain, clarify, and sell in order to persuade her audience that her plan for the company was the right one:

- By straying from our core strength – customer service and satisfaction – we have lowered our guard against the sleeping giants who are gearing up to compete ferociously with us.

- Our success, if not our survival, demands that we address our customer satisfaction problems now.

- To solve these problems, we must invest in a new customer service software solution and train everyone to use it.

- Software alone won't solve our problems. We must also refocus on customer satisfaction by monitoring and measuring our success in that area – and rewarding ourselves and our employees accordingly.

- At the same time, we must not become overly cautious as individuals or as a company. Bold entrepreneurship has been a key ingredient of our success. Now we need to create a culture of "disciplined entrepreneurship," encouraging new ideas and initiatives that serve our customer-centric goals.

- The money we invest in this plan will be recovered within the first 16 months after the plan is in place.

Note that this leader did not end up with a strict point-by-point correspondence between her lists of obstacles and messages. The message discovery process is not that tidy, nor should it be. You'll probably come up with a whole laundry list of key messages. And then you will prioritize and reduce them into compelling messages.

The president of a nonprofit institution develops a fundraising speech.

Together with a speechwriter, I worked with the president of a religious studies consortium to develop a fundraising speech. The objective was simple and clear: *I want them to contribute money to the consortium.*

But in a briefing with the president and his staff, we identified a number of formidable obstacles.

Persuading people to give money to your nonprofit organization is a tricky business. Beyond making sure that your audience understands what you do and why it matters, you have to give them that all-important sense of "what's in it for me." And you have to make them feel a sense of urgency about your mission or your cause; otherwise, it's all too easy for them to go away and forget about you.

A museum or arts organization can boast about its programs and performances and offer perks like special events and priority access for donors. A medical foundation or relief organization can point to the lives it saves or the people it helps. But for an academic institution like this one, which is devoted to advanced education and research in a wide range of religions, the challenges are more daunting.

We listed the obstacles in the form of questions that would have to be addressed at least implicitly in the speech:

What is the consortium? What does it do? What does it stand for?

- As an academic institution, isn't the consortium something of an "ivory tower?" What does it have to do with "real-world" problems – or solutions to those problems?

- I'm a Catholic/Lutheran/Jew/Buddhist/Muslim/etc. Why should I support the consortium instead of an institution associated with my own faith?

- The consortium has been around for a long time and is well-established; why does it need or merit my support now?

- The consortium was founded in the 1960s and is associated with a university known for its liberalism. If it has a political agenda I find disagreeable, why should I support it?

Clearly, some of these questions represented basic obstacles of understanding; others were more complicated. Note, in particular, that the last was one of those issues that lurks below the surface, one of those questions of "What's really going on here?" that I mentioned earlier in this chapter.

Based on these questions, we formulated the following key messages:

- Today it seems that people are more divided than ever by religious differences. From urgent debates in medicine, law, and education to bigotry and fanaticism, religious issues and conflicts plague our communities, our society, and the nations of the world.

- Through its unique mission – fostering advanced religious research and training in an interfaith environment – the consortium promotes dialogue and understanding among peoples and cultures of different religions.

- The consortium attracts unique individuals and prepares them for leadership not only in religious and academic institutions but beyond, in service to their communities, society, and the world.

You should even address obstacles that lurk below the surface.

- The consortium has no political agenda except to rescue religious thought and discourse from the shrill rhetoric and polarizing politics that exploit religious issues for partisan purposes.

- The consortium is a place where religion meets the world, and the training, commitment, and service of our graduates make the world a better place.

In this instance, framing the questions that could be expected to form in the minds of the audience was somewhat speculative. After all, this was to be a stump speech, something the president of the consortium could use with various audiences. So the audience was considerably more of an unknown quantity than the health food company leader faced in her high-stakes meeting with her own senior management team.

And yet the technique – anticipate the obstacles, then decide what you need to say to overcome them – worked just as effectively to discover and define the messaging foundation for the fundraising speech.

✔

The preparation protocol plots a course for the future!

The Importance of Preparation

Sometimes I run into clients who resist the preparation protocol. They feel quite sure they know what they want to say, and they don't see any point in taking the time to go over it or delve into it. In the end, these clients profit from the preparation process every bit as much as – and sometimes more than – those who start out with only vague ideas of what they want to say.

In my experience, effective leaders invest substantial time and energy in message discovery. Often, this is because they look beyond the event they're preparing for. They may be plotting a new course for their organization, like the health food executive. They may be kicking off an extended communications campaign, like the president of the religious studies consortium.

Or they may be formulating an entire strategy for their enterprise, like one of the savviest clients I've coached.

> Every other year, this CEO hosted a three-day conference for his biggest customers and partners – a very important event for his $350 million business. Together with a speechwriter, I had the privilege of working with him on his keynote address for this event a couple of times. At our kickoff meeting the second time around, the "briefing" we expected from this executive wandered far and wide. He speculated and theorized, mused and digressed, suggested ideas and tested ideas and rejected ideas – including some he had just suggested. The speechwriter tried to take notes, but pretty much gave up after a while (he was taping the discussion, anyway). Meanwhile, I was at the white board, trying to get down what I thought I was hearing and make some sort of order out of it. It wasn't a pretty picture. But it was teeming with ideas.

After a couple of hours we took a break, and when the client had left the room, the speechwriter turned to me in dismay. "I'm surprised he's so unprepared," he said of our client. "He seems to have no idea what he wants to say! What's the matter with him?"

I had known the client long enough to understand what he was up to. "We're not simply developing his speech for the conference," I explained. "He's using the speech to think through his plans for the business over the next two years."

How did I know this? For one thing, each time he returned from the customer conference, the first thing he did was deliver his keynote address to his own employees.

A compelling message takes you beyond the meeting.

Like great plays, compelling messages "have legs," as we say in the theater. They can carry you far beyond the speech, presentation, or high-stakes meeting you're preparing. Propagated through an organization, elaborated for various audiences, media, and events, they can become a campaign, a strategy, a recipe for success. But, just like good plays, great messages take time and effort to discover and develop.

Exercise: Preparation is the Key to Success.

Protocol for Developing a Strategic Message

Consider a presentation you have coming up, or one you expect to make (or would like to make) in the more distant future. Give yourself time to work your way through all the following questions.

By the end of this exercise, you'll not only "own" this technique for message discovery – you'll also have a blueprint of your presentation's key messaging.

Set the Context.

All communications take place in a context, made up of several elements; facts, trends, history, players, biases, "what's really going on." Because these circumstances will influence how you will be *heard*, you must take them into account as you develop what you plan to *say*.

Start by asking one big question: What is the context in which you will be delivering your presentation?

This is one big questions which really encompasses many smaller questions. Who is the audience? What are the economic circumstances? What is the competition doing? What issues are swirling around that impact your audience and their perception during your presentation?

Assess the Opportunities.

What are the opportunities you hope to exploit with this presentation? List the results you'll achieve if the presentation goes well …

Immediately? Within one month? In one year?

How will a successful presentation enhance your personal reputation, your company's fortunes, or your brand?

Assess the Risks.

What's at risk if your presentation goes poorly? Will your product fail … your initiative stall … your personal reputation, your company's fortunes, or your brand suffer?

What will it cost – in time, money, lost opportunities – to recover?

Exercise: Preparation is the Key to Success.

Who, Where and When?

Who is your audience?

Answer all the questions you can about them, including what they know and think about you (personally, as a leader or teacher, as the representative of a company or brand, etc.) and how that might prejudice or influence their response to you.

When are you presenting?

What time of day? More important, when in the history of your relationship with the audience? When in the budget cycle, the sales process, the merger, the history of your initiative, etc.?

Where is the presentation taking place?

In hostile, neutral, or friendly territory? In what kind of space (a conference room, an auditorium, or something in between) and with what kind of equipment (a stage and/or podium, A/V equipment, etc.)?

What are Your Objectives?

What exactly do you want from your audience? More specifically, what do you want them to believe or do? State your objective in an active sentence: I want them to:

What are the Obstacles?

Consider the obstacles to achieving your objective. Fear? Cost? Competition?

What are Your Key Messages?

List the proactive messages you have to get across in order to overcome the obstacles, answer the tough questions, and achieve your objective.

Exercise: Preparation is the Key to Success.

Step Back and Look for the Theme.

Now that you know your objective, the obstacles and your messages, it is time to consider a theme, or a mantra. Some examples to inspire you:

- *The Sweet Spot.*

- *Taking Advantage of Our Advantage.*

- *Doing Right and Doing Well.*

- *Continuous Innovation.*

- *The Best at Getting Better.*

Tough Questions

Anticipate three questions you don't want to answer.

Chapter 8

Structuring Your Presentation

Design to Win.

The previous chapters are about creating and using the tools and materials that go into an effective presentation: messages that have the fine, rich intensity of a master chef's sauce … Powerbites that drive your messages home like the sure, true blows of a hammer … and the ways you can use stories to bring your message and your mission to life and connect with the hearts and minds of your audience. Now, what's the most effective way to put them together?

The Importance of Structure

Consider the presentations you've attended. Think how often the speaker's idea of structure seemed to be "Start talking and go on and on until time runs out." Think of the PowerPoint presentations that ended in halting embarrassment as the speaker ran out of slides before running out of time or, for that matter, before making a point. Or – even worse – the presentations when the speaker ran out of time before running out of slides, and left the audience wondering, "What did we miss?"

Even when a speaker manages to deliver all the slides, at a consistent pace and within the allotted time, PowerPoint often lures a presentation into a linear procession to nowhere. The audience is treated to a succession of slides, adding up to a list of things that must be important – otherwise, they wouldn't have been featured on slides, right? The problem is, no one thing seems any more important than any other. There's no sense of progression, little emphasis, few logical signposts. The audience is left wondering, "What was the point?" (Of course, any presentation, PowerPoint or not, can drift. My point here is not to dump on PowerPoint. It can be a very useful tool, and, in any case, it's here to stay.)

Every audience wants structure. You might even say that, like children, every audience needs structure. In any case, as a presenter, you owe it to your audience to provide structure. Structure helps them listen and keeps them listening. Structure does more than enable you to organize your presentation; by helping your audience to organize your presentation in their minds, structure helps them understand and remember it.

Your audience deserves to know how you will use their precious time.

The structure of the beginning, middle and end: Say it, say it, say it.

This chapter is about structure, not content. Your particular purpose – exactly what you want to persuade your audience to believe or to do – will always drive the content of your presentation. A trial summation is different from a sales pitch is different from a press briefing is different from a conference keynote. For that matter, every trial summation, sales pitch, press briefing, and conference keynote is different from every other presentation of the same genre.

So I can't lay out some one-size-fits-all way to organize your thoughts. What I can offer is a foolproof blueprint for two of the three basic structural elements of a presentation: the beginning and the end. The middle, being the substance of what you have to say, is up to you. But the beauty of this approach is, even if you don't already have a thorough grasp of the substance of your presentation, this blueprint will both force you and help you to do so.

When we were learning to write, most of us were taught this fundamental way to organize an essay: Say what you're going to say … say it … then say what you've said. Tried and true, this is in fact the basis for my blueprint for effective presentations.

Open with the Hook, Promise and Roadmap.

As proverbial wisdom and our parents would have us remember, first impressions are powerful and persistent. So you will not be surprised to read that the opening of any presentation is crucial for several reasons.

The first five minutes are precious.

You never get a second chance to make a first impression.

First and foremost, this is the moment when your audience is most attentive. Research shows that people's attention is keenest during the first few minutes of a presentation. In as little as five minutes, that attention begins to sag – and then it usually goes downhill from there. You simply cannot afford to squander those first precious minutes. There is too much to accomplish during this short time.

Self-interest is compelling.

Your opening is your chance to capture the audience's attention and establish rapport with them. There is no more effective way to do that than to answer what I've identified, in an earlier module, as the foremost question in the minds of every audience: What's in it for me? You can define the answer in your opening or, more tantalizingly, suggest it. Either way, self-interest is the most powerful motivator in the world; by appealing to theirs, you will compel your audience to listen attentively to what you have to say.

A good opening tells them how to listen.

I believe it's just as important to outline or preview your presentation in your opening. By telling an audience where you're going and what to expect, you make them partners in the journey. In effect, you coach them in how to listen to your presentation.

Establish the message mantra.

Finally, the opening is a good time to establish your message mantra. Don't be afraid of "giving away the end" of your speech. Instead, remind yourself of the lamentable fact that many people are likely to leave the room before you reach your big conclusion; you don't want them to get away without hearing the single most important thing you want them to remember. Remember, too, that a key function of your message mantra is to unify your presentation in the minds of the audience. Like telling them what to expect, your message mantra serves the audience as an aid to listening and a foundation for understanding your entire presentation. To achieve these objectives, your opening needs to contain three essential elements that I call the hook, the promise, and the roadmap.

The Hook

It's all about one objective: seizing your audience's attention. The hook can come in any number of shapes and sizes. For example, you can cite and comment on a current news headline … ask a rhetorical question … unveil something new … present a unique visual … or share some unexpected or surprising data.

As you might expect, I tend to favor the storytelling hook, because of its power to capture not only the audience's attention but their imagination, too. I've seen storytelling work its magic in the opening of many presentations, including these:

> In an unforgettable debut before a national audience, a healthcare executive opened with the story of a pediatrician in his organization who was presented with a child in imminent danger from a difficult-to-diagnose heart condition. Masterfully composed and delivered, this compelling narrative captivated the audience while dramatizing all the key characteristics of the healthcare model the speaker advocated.

> The story followed the doctor as he rushed down the hall to consult with a specialist (integrated care) … used advanced computer search technology to diagnose the child's condition as a life-threatening emergency (technology innovation) … and called for a Medevac to transport the patient to a special facility (centers of excellence). The story ended on a heart-warming note as the doctor made his annual visit to his former patient's birthday party. In less than five minutes, the executive had the audience firmly in his grasp, as he went on to observe that there are thousands of such doctors and such stories in his organization, empowered by a healthcare model that delivers superior care while inspiring pride among the providers.

Hook them immediately, and you're more likely to keep them to the end.

*

I once worked with a client who was preparing a presentation for executives on professional ethics. For his hook, he decided to read, word for word, from a newspaper story. The risk of starting off by reading from a text – what could be duller? – was counterbalanced by the drama and authenticity of the story, which described in graphic, harrowing detail a prominent executive's fall from grace. Having captured the audience's attention, he then posed the question: "Could this happen to you?" Talk about a "what's-in-it-for-me" bombshell! From that moment, the speaker had the undivided attention of everyone in the room.

*

✔

Aspirational stories make great hooks.

Another client used an aspirational story – what I call "the nirvana hook" – to open a presentation on project management. He painted a vivid picture of a company succeeding, thriving, and growing by harnessing its business processes to a unique new model of project management. Having hooked his audience with this tantalizing slice of the organizational life of the future, the speaker had their full attention – and in the end, their buy-in – as he went on to describe how such "nirvana" could be achieved.

My final example of a compelling hook comes from a case of what I call presenting up – that is, making an internal presentation to your management.

A pair of business professionals was scheduled to appear before the executive committee of a large organization in order to secure final buy-in for a major technology project. A lot of groundwork had been done in the preceding months, and the pair was concerned they might open a Pandora's Box of issues if they reviewed the whole history and the many decisions that had led to this important moment.

With the blessing of their sponsor (always important when presenting up), they chose instead to open with a unique hook: they read a letter, supposedly from the executive committee itself to the entire company, announcing the committee's support for the initiative, outlining the reasons for it, and describing what would be expected of everyone in the organization in support of the project. This unique hook, which actually constituted pretty much the entire presentation, worked like a charm. After a few questions, the executive committee gave its blessing and thanked the pair of presenters for both the project and the brevity of the presentation.

What about using a joke as your hook? I strongly advise against it.

When Sir Donald Wolfit, a renowned British stage actor, was on his deathbed, a young colleague said to him, "Sir Donald, after a life so filled with success and fame, dying must be hard." "Dying is easy," replied the aged thespian, "comedy is hard."

If comedy is difficult for actors (and I can testify that it is), it's even harder for the average speaker. It's especially risky to try to be funny at the beginning of a presentation, before the audience has gleaned a sense of your personality, timing, and vocal style.

The rewards of opening with a joke, long shot that they are, hardly seem worth the risk. If your joke bombs, you can easily lose your audience for good, right out of the gate. And really, what's to be gained? "I'm a funny person" is an essential hook in a stand-up comedy routine. But rarely, if ever, will it be the first thing you need to establish in a business or professional presentation. Humor can be great for livening up a presentation or reviving an audience that's losing focus. But hold off on the jokes until you're relaxed and comfortable with your audience and they with you.

The Promise

Throw the gauntlet and give your explicit answer to the question, "What's in it for me?" By describing the insights, capabilities, and other benefits that the audience will gain from your presentation, you offer your commitment to the audience to repay them for listening – and you deepen their commitment to doing just that.

What's in it for me?

Here are a few opening promises used by clients I've worked with:

> "When we're finished, you'll have all the tools you need to make sound ethical judgments you can count on to protect you from litigation."

> "At the end of this presentation, you'll understand how a transformation of our organizational culture from technology-focused to entertainment-focused will guarantee our future."

> "My goal is to inspire you to share my enthusiasm for our doctor empanelment initiative. When you leave this room, you'll understand the quality-of-care benefits, you'll see how easy we make it for you to participate, and you'll appreciate how this initiative will enhance not only patient satisfaction, but your own as well"

> "Through this presentation I hope to persuade you how incredibly valuable it is to team with project management experts when pitching new commercial building clients."

The Roadmap

The roadmap serves as an agenda for the audience. The roadmap backs up the promise by outlining how you're going to fulfill it. By giving your audience a sense of the scope of the journey ahead and the route you plan to take, the roadmap allows them to buckle in more securely. By giving them an outline or preview of topics and ideas to listen for, the roadmap enables them to be better listeners.

The typical roadmap should be straightforward, short and simple. Here are three examples I've heard in my practice:

> "First, we'll survey the legal landscape. Then I'll offer you some tools to calibrate your ethical compass. Finally, we'll work through a few compelling case studies.

> "I first want to frame this issue in the context of our other quality and service initiatives. Then I'll show you some compelling data on the impact of improved access. Next, I'll describe our initiative in detail, with special attention to your role. And finally, I'll show you how far this initiative can go in improving your long-term satisfaction."

> "My roadmap is simple. First, I'll show how we can sweeten the pitch. Next, we'll describe some examples of how we can accelerate every project, which means getting you to your commission faster. Finally, we'll explore various ways of deepening and extending your relationship with the client."

The Roadmap tells us what to expect.

The Body Follows the Roadmap.

As the examples illustrate, the roadmap is a summary. With the roadmap, you say what you're going to say. Then, of course, you say it, which is the core of your presentation. That's what makes the roadmap such a valuable tool for you as well as the audience. And you can use this tool in more than one way, depending on how you go about preparing your presentation.

If you haven't already planned and organized what you're going to say, composing your roadmap will force you to do so. In effect, you'll use the roadmap as an outline.

Or you may flesh out the core of your presentation first. Then preparing your roadmap can serve as a checkpoint. Summarizing your presentation in the simple, straightforward, and brief form of a roadmap is a great way to verify that it's clear, coherent, and complete.

The Close: "Say What You've Said."

The close is not just the end – it's your chance to close the deal with your audience.

In the close, you connect all the dots. You drive home your message mantra. And you issue a call to action – at least a call to believe – to your audience.

During the close, according to the old essay-writing blueprint, you say what you've said. To do that – and to accommodate the inevitable latecomers who may have missed your brilliant opening and even part of the core of your presentation – I recommend a simple strategy: recapitulate the key elements of your opening.

Return to the Hook.

By returning to the hook you used in the opening, you can unify your presentation and give the audience a sense of closure. A few examples:

> "And so we return to Maria, the patient whose story opened this presentation. Hers is just one story of the huge difference our new model of patient care can make. And I trust you believe, just as I do, that this is just the beginning ..."

> "I opened today by reading you a newspaper headline that chronicled the devastation of a career just like yours. With the knowledge and tools I've shared with you here, I believe you can make sure you are never the subject of such a news story."

> "One memorable day on a mountain, it took a team to rescue my father-in-law from the crevasse that threatened to be his grave. Not a single hero, but all the climbers on that mountain, working together – just as, together, we can take this enterprise to the next level."

Restate the Promise.

By reminding your audience of the promise, you lay it on the line. You say, in effect, "I made a promise and I'm not afraid to repeat it because I'm confident that I've delivered." Some examples:

> "I promised when I began today that by the end of the session, you would share my enthusiasm for this initiative ... that you would see the huge impact it will have on the quality of our care and service ... and that you would understand how easy it will be for you to participate."

> "I promised you earlier that I was going to show you how changing our focus from a technology-driven platform to an entertainment-driven platform will ensure our future and guarantee our success."

> "I promised that you would see the immense benefit of teaming with project management as you engage clients seeking new commercial facilities."

Use the close to connect the dots.

Review the Roadmap.

Reviewing the roadmap is a succinct way to say what you've said in the core of your presentation. For example:

> "You've come to understand and appreciate the hazards of the climate you work in. You've heard about the latest in both case law and policies and procedures. You've done a helpful self-assessment

of vulnerabilities. I've shared with you some strategies, tactics, and tips you can apply today. And along the way, we've been able to look in detail at some compelling case studies as a means of sharpening both your awareness and your skills."

"I've laid out the reasons our competitiveness and success depend on our quality and service initiatives. You've seen some compelling data on the impact of improved access. You understand the details of our newest initiative and of your role. Finally, I trust you now see how empanelment will secure our long-term future as physicians."

✔

People tune in again when they know the end is near.

Signal the end.

There's one more reason to invoke any or all of the elements that made up your opening when you're drawing things to a close. Doing so is a great way to signal the audience that you – and they – are approaching the end. Signaling them that you're "finishing up" will almost always revive the flagging spirits and sharpen the attention of an audience. But always take special care as you approach the end of your presentation. If you tip off the audience too soon that you're coming to a close, they may start to pack up and psychically or physically leave the room. On the other and, if you put in several "false endings" – that is, indicate that you're concluding a number of times without actually doing so – you're likely to annoy your audience and leave them with the impression that you're a windbag.

Make It Yours.

Every speech or presentation is unique, as it should be. In the end, how you organize it has to work for you, for the occasion and purpose of the presentation, and, of course, for your audience. I've called the ideas in this module a blueprint, but you should consider them a rough drawing.

As I've noted, for example, there are all kinds of ways to hook an audience. Oftentimes, the promise and the roadmap can easily be combined – indeed, sometimes it only makes sense to combine them. On some occasions, the whole point may be to build to a big announcement, a dramatic conclusion, or a surprise; in these cases you won't want to give anything away, so you'll omit the promise or the roadmap altogether.

Similarly, it's up to you to use, arrange, and emphasize the elements of your close in the way that works best. Weaving together the return to the hook, the promise, and the roadmap is an art. And as with any art, you want your audience to experience the art and not the technique. Sometimes it may make sense to bring in something altogether new at the close – new information or a fresh story or anecdote – in order to make your close that much more compelling.

And so in structuring this module, I return to the beginning. Structure does more than enable you to organize your presentation; by helping your audience to organize your presentation in their minds, structure helps them understand and remember it.

PowerPoint and Beyond

Often I have clients ask me how to structure their PowerPoint presentations. The first thing I ask is, "Why PowerPoint?"

Are you sure PowerPoint is the best vehicle to tell your story?

More Effective Ways to Highlight Key Points

PowerPoint is the official go-to method of presentation, which means it is also an overused medium. PowerPoint presentations can cue the audience that it's time to snooze. I always challenge my clients to think beyond PowerPoint to more effective ways to illustrate key messages in the presentations. Consider these methods as an alternative:

Use the white board.

The white board allows you to actively illustrate your point so your audience can engage with you.

Post key visuals.

Blow up the few pictures that illustrate your key points and refer to them during the course of your presentation.

Paint a picture with a story.

Use storytelling to capture their attention and take them with you onto your journey. It can also be very effective to begin your presentation with a story, and use the PowerPoint deck within the body of the presentation.

PowerPoint Rules: Make it Presentable!

If you must include PowerPoint slides in your presentation, your goal is to make the slides support your presentation. You are the star of the show and the PowerPoint is there to help you drive home your key messages. Here are my recommendations:

Data slides

Design simple, compelling data slides. You will provide the interpretation of the data in your presentation.

It can be useful to create detailed slides for your appendices. If you really engage your audience during the presentation, you can always dive into those slides for a more in-depth discussion.

Text slides and the rule of three

Limit the text to emphasize key pieces of information. Always follow the rule of three:

- Make your key message the title

- Use no more than three bullets per slide.

- Use no more than three words in each bullet. If you have images to illustrate each bullet, use them.

When it comes to getting in front of an audience, you will want to support your presentation with a PowerPoint deck that promotes presenting.

"Send Me the Deck."

One version persuades a live audience.

An alternate persuades by email.

In the PowerPoint culture, there are decision-makers, leaders and customers who will say, "Send me the deck." The deck you send them is a written version of your presentation designed to persuade someone who does not get to engage with you live. PowerPoint is a good tool when used this way. If you anticipate that your key audiences will ask for a deck, then you should build two versions of your presentation. One of your presentations will support your live presentation, where your talk track and a few compelling visuals will drive the persuasion. The other will be designed as a complete written persuasion similar to a "white paper."

As a presenter, you owe it to yourself and your audience to provide structure. Besides facilitating the development of your messages, effective tools like the Hook, Promise and Roadmap help you engage your listeners and set their expectations for a high impact, memorable journey. Structure is the backbone to your successful persuasions.

Chapter 9

Rehearsal Techniques

How Do You Get to Carnegie Hall?

A kid carrying a violin case walks up to a policeman in New York City.

"Officer," the kid says, "how do I get to Carnegie Hall?"

The cop replies, "Practice, practice, practice."

"Practice, practice, practice."

Musicians, actors, and dancers rehearse for countless hours, both alone and with their ensembles. So do athletes and sports teams – they call it practice instead of rehearsal. For months before lift-off, space shuttle crews undergo a long course of rigorous training that includes meticulous rehearsals of each crucial operation of their mission. Armed forces rehearse endlessly, from training raw troops in basic combat operations to doing "dry runs" of planned operations. These and many other professions have a tradition of rehearsal – no questions asked – it's simply a given that the way to success is practice, practice, practice.

So it baffles me that so many business and professional presentations are given with little or no rehearsal. When I see someone make a speech that obviously wasn't rehearsed much, if at all, I ask myself, did he think the stakes were too low to justify the time it would take to practice, even just a little?

When are the stakes high enough to make it worth your while to rehearse?

When there's an audience you care about.

Here's one answer: The stakes are high enough when there is an audience you care about and when you are taking up their precious time. Unrehearsed presentations, like the first draft of a piece of writing, tend to be long, flabby, repetitive, disjointed, and ultimately boring. Are you really willing to try the patience of your audience with such a performance? Why would you want to risk alienating them when your purpose is to persuade them?

When you care about your reputation.

Here's another answer: Every presentation you give in business and professional life shapes your reputation, your "personal brand." Are you okay with gaining a reputation for being tedious, confusing, or confused? Worse, are you willing to risk the joke that bombs, the quip that offends, the phrase that poisons the air for you, your company, your project, your purpose? Those are the mistakes that unrehearsed speakers make.

Invest in rehearsal to become a better persuader.

Even if you know the material forwards and backwards.

In addition to the granddaddy of all excuses – "There wasn't time" – I commonly hear a couple of other reasons why people don't rehearse.

"I know this material backwards and forwards ... I've given this presentation before ... believe me, it just flows." When I hear this as a coach, I immediately have two concerns - Is it possible that what this person considers as "flow" will be what the audience considers as "canned?" Does knowing the material cold really absolve the presenter from continuously improving and refreshing his content and performance? The last time he presented this material he "knows cold," was it well-organized and well-paced? Powerful and persuasive? Not too long and not too short for the allotted time? The last time he presented this material, did the audience give the same high marks he is giving himself by suggesting that rehearsal is unnecessary?

And even if you can think on your feet.

"Don't worry, I'm good thinking on my feet." If you're good at thinking on your feet, you have an admirable skill. But I have an announcement: thinking-on-your-feet presentations are almost always inferior to those that are well and truly rehearsed. To invoke the analogy with writing one more time, how many first drafts have you written that didn't get better through revision and polishing?

Preparation fuels spontaneity.

I've also encountered people who sincerely believe that rehearsal makes them flat, fake or stale. "But what about my spontaneity?" they ask. Most people don't rehearse enough to make their presentation flat. And those who do make a presentation flat through rehearsal are probably using the wrong rehearsal techniques.

Effective rehearsal actually helps to build confidence and relaxation. The confident, relaxed presenter is far more likely to listen to the audience, adjust the message and offer spontaneous insights or observations during a well-rehearsed presentation.

Scripted presentations require more rehearsal.

I often encounter presenters who believe a script gives them permission to skip rehearsal. With a heavily scripted presentation (especially one reviewed to within an inch of its life by the legal department), you start at a disadvantage. Others have chosen your words for you. Not only must you become familiar with their words, you must also "make them your own" so you can deliver them in a natural, relaxed, conversational style. Which means that this kind of presentation actually requires more rehearsal, not less.

Now that I've worn out my soapbox, I'll share what I believe is the number one, perfectly understandable reason people don't rehearse business and professional presentations – They don't know how.

That's what this chapter is about: efficient, effective techniques for preparing powerful, persuasive presentations through rehearsal.

✔

Most people don't know how to rehearse.

Rehearse Out Loud and On Your Feet.

Don't just rehearse in your head. Simply reading over your script or your notes won't get you where you need to go. You have to rehearse a speech out loud and, assuming that you're going to be delivering it standing up, that's how you need to rehearse it – on your feet. Even if you'll be presenting in a sit-down environment, like a panel discussion, you'll greatly energize yourself and your performance by rehearsing on your feet.

Ideally, you should rehearse under conditions as close as possible to those in which you'll be presenting. You may not have access to an auditorium or a stage, but try at least to find a large space that will require you to project, vocally and physically. And of course, bring along an audience of at least one trusted colleague or friend, to give you objective feedback.

Rehearse in Sections.

Rehearsing is like going to the gym, the dance studio, or the driving range. It's a place to work on your strength, your skills, and your game under conditions free of performance pressure. It's a time to try new ideas and techniques, take risks, make discoveries. In my experience, it can and should be great fun and enormously exciting, as over and over you find yourself making significant breakthroughs in both content and style while rehearsing.

When approaching rehearsal, keep in mind you can't rehearse everything at once, much less polish and improve everything. You can't test your objectives, reassess the obstacles, revamp the structure, tinker with your rhetoric, smooth out the flow, work on your vocal skills, and perfect your movements and gestures all at the same time.

Most people, I've found, tend to want to start the rehearsal process with a complete run-through of their presentation. I advise against this. Trying to slog through an entire presentation right out of the gate is exhausting and inefficient. In all likelihood, you won't even get through the first half before you run out of time or energy or both. Maybe that's why so many presentations start strong, then drift and finish weak.

Instead, I recommend rehearsing distinct elements of a presentation, one at a time, then assembling the elements into a complete, polished whole.

First and Most, Rehearse the Opening and the Close.

We are most attentive at the beginning and the end.

As I emphasize in Chapter 8 and elsewhere, the opening and the close are the most important parts of any presentation. The opening is your chance – maybe your only chance – to seize command of the occasion and the attention of the audience. The close is what's most likely to be remembered, and your last chance to drive home your message and your call to action.

Right there, you have two big reasons to rehearse your opening and your close first and most. But there's another reason, especially if you've structured your presentation as recommended in Chapter 8, using a hook, a promise, and a roadmap as your opening, and then closing with a recapitulation of the same elements. By rehearsing the opening and close, you effectively rehearse the body of your whole presentation. If you've incorporated your message mantra into both the opening and the close, you also get a chance to work on that important statement. If you've heightened your rhetoric for the opening and the close, which is a common and very effective tactic, you get a chance to hear how it sounds and dial it up or down to a level that's comfortable.

There's one more reason to rehearse your opening and close first and most: if that's all you have time to rehearse, you'll be better prepared to give the entire presentation.

You'll have maximized the benefit of your rehearsal time. In a pinch – if you have, say, only an hour or two to rehearse – always spend at least half your rehearsal time on your opening and your close.

Sharpen Your Hook and Close with a Bang.

How often have you sat through an opening like this?

> Thank you … um, George. Thanks for, uh, those kind words of introduction. Um – let's see … just – get this – thing adjusted [amplified sound of buffeting microphone]. Okay. Now. What an event, huh? And what a place? What I want to do is, I want to start out by telling you a story – heh heh. It starts like this …

In the theater, this is called bleeding. An actor can bleed into a moment or out of one (or both); either way, bleeding drains the life out of the drama, by exhausting the patience of the audience before the moment unfolds or undermining the moment's significance by letting it drift away. In the same way, bleeding can also deal a mortal blow to a presentation, especially at the opening.

Here are my basic tips and techniques for rehearsing the two most important elements of any presentation – the things you should be sure you get right in your opening and close.

Go right for the hook.

My recommendation: Go right for the hook. Do not mention the occasion, the venue, or (heaven forbid) the weather. Acknowledge the person who introduced you (if any) or the applause that greeted you (if any) with a simple "Thank you." Then get on with it.

Let nothing get in the way. Go directly and immediately for the hook. And make it crisp. Some examples:

> "Thank you. *New York Times*, August 13th, 2004. Headline: 'HCA Executive Faces Criminal Probe. Indictment Expected.' The lead paragraph: 'The New York state attorney general will bring evidence this week to the grand jury …'"

*

> "Two months and five days ago, accompanied by an experienced wilderness guide, my father-in-law and I had just completed a glorious if arduous ascent up Mount Shasta – 14,162 feet above the floor of far Northern California. As we started to make our way down again, I took the lead – but after just a few minutes, I heard a strange sound from behind. I turned around to find that my father-in-law had disappeared."

*

> "A transformation is upon us. It's everywhere. Even in something as simple [holding out his hand] as this wristwatch I'm wearing or the sunglasses on my head. Pretty much since I started wearing watches, I've counted on them to give me the time. And I've counted on my sunglasses to shade my eyes. When the transformation I'm talking about is complete, I'll be able to count on wearable digital devices to give me a world of timely information and entertainment."

Close with a bang.

It's just as important to finish strong as it is to open strong. And it's just as possible to let a close bleed off into boredom or insignificance. You don't want your audience to leave, physically or psychically, before you've finished.

I believe it's a good idea to give the audience a cue that you are "wrapping up"; by showing them a light at the end of the tunnel, you can actually sharpen their attention on your closing. But if you say things like "And finally" more than once or twice, or tell them pleadingly that you're "almost finished," your close will start

The first three to five minutes are the money time.

People perk up for the close... so make it strong!

to hemorrhage. The audience will start to feel that you're never going to finish, and they'll start to tune you out.

Oddly enough, the same thing will happen if you begin to hurry your close because you're running out of time. The audience will sense that you've given up on your close, if not your entire presentation, and they'll give up on it, too.

With a well-rehearsed close, you can treat your audience to something akin to the stirring last movement of a symphony. That's why it's important to rehearse your close early and often, so you can bring fresh energy and gusto to it, just as you will want to do in performance. Be sure to keep up the pace, but try varying the rhythm and cadence as well as your volume. Try adding a "pregnant pause" before a significant point or a transition. Discover and practice the gestures you can use to underline key words and phrases, animate your feelings, and draw your audience to you. Try to end in one of your money positions.

Dare to wait for the applause.

Be sure to include the moment after you finish as part of your rehearsal, just as you should do in performance. Too often, presenters "cut and run" the instant they finish, as if they're relieved to be done or apologetic for taking the audience's time.

Instead, stand in there; the stage is still yours, so hold it a moment longer. By and large, an audience wants to show its appreciation for a job well done. So dare to wait for the applause. Sure, it doesn't always come, but when it does, accept it graciously. You and your audience will both feel more fulfilled.

Rehearse for Story Arc.

The story arc of your presentation is more than an outline (although it is that, too). It is your throughline, the driving train of information and logic that gives your presentation both momentum and coherence. When you consider presentations as a storytelling journey, you can start to establish sign posts along the way to keep you on track while propelling you to the next important element of your persuasion.

Rehearsing the arc enables you to see how all the sign posts of your presentation (and all the slides of your PowerPoint deck) fit together. At the same time, it puts you in touch with the importance and urgency of each of your objectives in turn. By helping you spot and expunge unnecessary tangents or forays into minutiae, rehearsing for story arc also helps you tighten up your presentation.

Just as in other kinds of rehearsal, it's important to be on your feet and say the words out loud when rehearsing the arc. But when you rehearse the arc, you don't rehearse the words you'll use in your presentation. Instead, for every PowerPoint slide, sign post, or key message, you simply state out loud what you intend to achieve. Here are three examples of rehearsing the arc:

A presentation without slides

- I'll start by establishing the consumer's yearning for the connected entertainment experience.

- I'll define what connected entertainment means to me, personally.

- I'll use my personal story to suggest that a tipping point is at hand.

- Next, I'll establish the three things we'll achieve with our newest innovations –

    1. weave together content and devices,

    2. extend these experiences beyond personal enjoyment to enjoyment with a broader community, and

    3. vastly expand both the range of entertainment experiences and the community that enjoys them.

- I'll demonstrate the games, the live service, the expanding community, and the ability to reach out and capture movies, television, and music.

- Finally, I'll return to the tipping point theme and suggest that the launch of these innovations will accelerate our growth from a competitive option to a ubiquitous presence in digital entertainment.

In rehearsing the arc, or the story line, you find weak spots.

A basic slide-by-slide presentation

Slide 1: Deliver the hook, promise, and roadmap.

Slide 2: Capture the imagination by describing the "nirvana experience."

Slide 3: Show the current pain points.

Slide 4: Establish our pedigree – we have the DNA to do this.

Slide 5: The message here is that we have the right structure.

Slide 6: Sell the leadership team – use stories.

Slide 7: Define the investment we'll need to make.

Slide 8: The key message: these investments have paid off before.

… and so forth.

A slide presentation with distinct sections

Section 1: The first slides establish the idea of the "burning platform." Here I'll use compelling data and one good story to create the sense of urgency.

Slide 1: Says our growth is slowing.

Slide 2: Shows our inefficiencies versus the market.

Slide 3: Shows the scary emergence of our competition.

Slide 4: This pivot slide asks the question: What is to be done?

Section 2: The next three slides are designed to give the audience hope that we can take distinct actions to turn the tide in our favor.

Slide 1: Proves the market is still immense.

Slide 2: Shows potential trajectory of our newest product.

Slide 3: Shows impact my efficiency initiative will have on productivity.

Section 3: With the next three slides, I'll go deeper into the staffing, resources, and timelines of our three initiatives.

Slide 1: Provides a compelling description of the growth campaign.

Slide 2: Takes a deep dive into the alignment of incentives initiative.

Slide 3: Convinces folks we have a great product innovation roadmap.

Section 4: The next two slides are all about actions.

Slide 1: Timelines, roles, and responsibilities for rollout of initiatives.

Slide 2: Calls the audience to action.

Close: The final slide paints a picture of our bright future once we've executed on our plan.

Get the story arc down cold to stay on track.

Although it may seem straightforward and even a bit dull, I cannot overemphasize the importance of rehearsing the story arc. I've seen it work magic for countless clients. Spreading printouts of a slide show on a conference room table and using them to rehearse the arc seems to sear the objectives and flow of the presentation into your brain. And don't underestimate the power of having your story arc down cold. When it comes time to make your presentation, it will help you keep up your pace, it will enable you to get right back on track when people interrupt or ask questions, and it will make you far more compelling and persuasive.

Rehearse the Problem Sections.

Once you've worked on your opening and close and gotten comfortable with the arc of your presentation, the next best use of your rehearsal time is to focus on those sections that need the most attention.

Chances are you'll know what your problem sections are, and your rehearsal audience can help you identify them as well. Your problem sections may be the most complex and therefore the most potentially confusing to your audience (if not to you). They may contain the most controversial or disruptive things you plan to say. They may be the new parts you've added to material you've presented before. They may not be "problem" sections so much as important sections that you want to be sure you have mastered.

Whatever the case, identify your problem sections and rehearse them, one at a time, until you're confident that you've got them down cold.

Vocal Rehearsal

By rehearsing your presentation verbatim as much as possible, you do more than "get used to" saying the words (although that is no small thing). You also get to experiment, to take risks, to make mistakes and make discoveries.

Review Chapter 10, "The Power of Voice." In vocal rehearsal, you want to work on your projection and articulation. Ask your rehearsal audience to sit in the back row. Can they hear and understand every word from back there? Don't forget to ask for their help in eliminating verbal tics like "um" or "uh," "okay" or "well." Make sure they bust you for saying "kinda" and "sorta," for starting sentences with "Basically," and for overusing empty, overused adjectives like "amazing" and "incredible."

Work on varying your volume, pitch, pace, and cadence to support the content of your presentation. Don't hold back; by trying out bold vocal choices, you'll often discover your best stuff.

Physical Rehearsal

Good public speakers make their audiences comfortable by being comfortable themselves – comfortable in their own skins; that is, physically comfortable in their bodies and in the space they occupy. That's why physical rehearsal is important.

Physical rehearsal is your chance to decide what you are going to do with your body during your presentation. Sit or stand? Where? How? Move from one place to another? When? How? If you're using PowerPoint, determine how to position yourself so the audience can focus on you at one moment and be easily directed to the screen at another. And of course, you'll need to make sure you avoid staring at or standing in front of the screen.

Do the tone and physical life complement the message you're sending?

Your Entrance

Practice your entrance. If that sounds silly, remember that you are an actor, a performer in your own show, and first impressions are crucial. How you enter from "nowhere" to "here" will be the first thing that shapes their perception of you and your presentation. Your entrance will set the tone for your presentation and shape your audience's perception of you.

Staging

Commit one of your rehearsals to staging – where you stand, when and where you move, your body language and gestures. Establish your "money" positions – three distinct places in the performance space where you look powerful (and where you can be seen and heard by everyone, of course), discussed in Chapter 10 – and put them to use during your all-important opening and close.

Rehearse the arc of your presentation with your focus on the staging. Decide what sections you'll present from each of your money positions, and figure out when and how you'll move from one to another. The idea is to add variety to what the audience is watching – you. Nothing commands an audience's attention like movement, but as I emphasize in Chapter 10, you don't want to wander aimlessly. Your movements must have "definition" – start, go, stop. That doesn't mean you have to rush, and it doesn't mean you should stop talking as you move. Indeed, a speaker "on a stroll," who can walk and talk and maintain rapport with an audience all at the same time, is a speaker that audiences cannot ignore.

Gestures

Spend some time working on your gestures. Here again, you'll need the help and feedback of your rehearsal audience. Are there parts of your presentation that would benefit from more animation? What kind of gestures work best for you and best for your most important moments? Try out various gestures to see how they work for you and your audience.

Meanwhile, root out your physical tics. Are you fidgeting with your pen, staring off into space when you pause for breath, swaying when you stand? Urge your rehearsal audience to be ruthless in pointing out such faults.

Finally, be sure to practice with the tools and technologies you'll be using, if any: microphone and microphone stand, remote control, laser pointer, overhead projector, flip chart, mouse, controller, whatever.

Find energy in an Italian run-through

Italian Run-through

There's an old theater tradition called the Italian run-through, in which the actors zip through the dialogue at double or triple normal speed, often indulging in big, over-the-top gestures and emotions at the same time. I recommend that you make this exercise part of your vocal rehearsal, especially if you have a tendency to be too deliberate or to speak in a steady, even tone, which audiences find boring. Aside from being lots of fun for you and your rehearsal audience, doing an Italian run-through will unleash reserves of energy you didn't know you have. You'll probably be surprised at just how many over-the-top elements your audience tells you to "keep in." You may find yourself taking your presentation to an entirely new level.

After Rehearsal, Before Showtime

Don't confuse rehearsal with performance.

Rehearsal tends to be a technical process, requiring you to focus on specific elements of your presentation and performance – the open and close, structure, posture, movement, voice, gesture, and all the rest. You'll probably find yourself watching yourself during rehearsals. In the theater, we call this the "third eye." A helpful if not essential tool, it's the awareness of how you look and sound that enables you to shape and improve your presentation. But it's dangerous, too, because it can seduce you into a kind of self-consciousness that can undermine your performance.

As you move from rehearsal to performance, shrink the third eye. Put your concerns about technique out of your mind, and have faith that the practice you've put in will "be there" for you at showtime.

Are they getting the message?

During performance, your primary concern must be "Are they getting the message?" Not "How am I doing?" or "Do they like me?" Remember, the most important person in the room is not you … it's your audience. Focus on them, and talk with them. Keep it simple. Stay with your objectives. Hold your message mantra close. And let all the "technical" stuff take care of itself.

From rehearsal to performance!

To get to Carnegie Hall, every kid with a violin has to practice, practice, practice. Once she arrives on that great stage, however, her job is not to show off her technique. Her job is to move the audience by artfully performing the music. Like great musicians, great presenters forget all about rehearsal when it's showtime. They trust that all the preparation they've done will stand them in good stead. They know their job is to deliver artfully a presentation that will engage, inspire and persuade.

Manage the third eye when you're on stage.

Exercise: Verbal Tics and How to Cure Them

Verbal tics keep you from communicating effectively.

"Umm ... uh ... like ... you know"

We've, umm, all sat through the, you know, kind of presentation that gets, like, unbearable because the speaker just can't, you know, stop sticking umms and uhs and likes and other junk into every sentence or idea. These habitual verbal tics are sometimes rooted in problems with content, preparation, or confidence. But if you're afflicted, you need not despair – there is a cure.

Enlist an audience to signal your tics.

Sit down with a trusted friend, colleague, or family member and start talking. You can run through a presentation you've done before, describe your plans for one you have coming up, or just talk about a recent event. But before you begin, make a contract with your audience of one that he or she will interrupt with a loud buzzing sound or snap of the fingers every time you say "umm" or "you know" or the like.

Learn to replace each tic with a brief pause.

Warning: As you're interrupted again and again, you will be aghast at how often you fall back on your tics. You may get upset, even angry, and lose your train of thought more than once. But keep at it. As your awareness of them grows, so will your concentration on suppressing your tics. You'll find that you need to slow down and think ahead. At first, you will probably have to "stop yourself" and replace each "umm" and "uh" with a brief pause.

Practice!

Break down what you're saying into units, or sets of ideas, and try to get through one at a time without a single tic. You'll soon be on your way to success. But don't rely on a single such session to cure you. You must remain vigilant about your tic. Ask those you trust to remind you when you slip. You should be able to completely purge your communications of all verbal tics in three to six weeks.

Chapter 10

The Power of the Voice

Great Voices Capture the Imagination.

The most compelling public speakers, the best actors, the greatest "pitch" masters, all have one thing in common: great use of the voice.

Voices vary infinitely, and the one nature gave you is the one you have to work with. You may not be blessed with the great "pipes" of a Richard Burton or a Lauren Bacall, but no matter; you can use the voice you have to great effect. In talking, as in most everything else, there are certain techniques for getting the most out of your natural ability.

Vocalization is a physical, even athletic activity, and like any sport, it can take many hours of practice and years of experience to master. Just as you can't learn to sing by reading music, you can't develop your vocal style and power by simply reading about vocal techniques.

If your goal is to change your voice, I recommend combining this guide with a vocal warm-up and workout regimen. I offer a short series of vocal warm-up and workout exercises; follow along with the Change Your Voice, Change Your Life video series on my You Tube channel at youtube.com/butterfieldpofp.

Power your voice for a powerful persuasion.

Activating Your Voice

Just as we often speak of the quality of a voice as its "color" or "character," we employ even more elaborate metaphorical language to describe voices. How would you describe your best friend's voice, or your spouse's, or your own? Is it bright or breathy, silky or smoky, smooth or raw, resonant or reedy, bell-like or booming? The fundamental distinction is weak or strong. Strong is better; no matter what the inherent character of your voice, you always bring out its best qualities, and sound more confident and more persuasive, by using it vigorously. In the theater, this is called projection.

Mindful Breathing

Projection is more than just a matter of how loud you are. A good actor or speaker can actually lower his or her voice (or at least seem to) and be heard in the farthest row of the balcony. Projection is a matter of supporting your voice with your breath. It comes from your diaphragm, the musculature that operates your lungs. That's why it's important to be aware of your breathing when you're speaking in public. Being mindful of your breathing will help you take deep, full breaths, which will in turn keep you from hurrying your speech and running out of breath. Before long, you'll get in the habit of supporting your voice with good breathing, and it will become natural to you.

Projection is also a matter of where your voice comes from inside your head, throat, and chest. In general, the further "back" a voice comes from, the more it fills the oral cavity and throat, the more strongly it will project.

One of the first tips budding actors and performers learn: Always talk to the last row of the audience. Making a conscious effort to do so will automatically improve your projection.

✔

Give value to the words by pronouncing them correctly.

Bring Focus to Your Sound Through Articulation.

Americans are notoriously lazy speakers. This is not just a matter of how idiomatic and slangy our modern American version of English has become. Much of the crispness of traditional English pronunciation has gone by the wayside in our everyday communications. (Of course, if you learn a foreign language from a textbook or a bunch of audio tapes, then visit the country where it's spoken, you'll probably think the native speakers are a tribe of mushmouths, too.)

You can't deliver an effective presentation – people will simply stop paying attention to you – if you can't be understood. Pronouncing words clearly, known as articulation or diction, is essential to your power of persuasion. The kind of lazy talking we can get away with in our personal and everyday communications – the consonants soft and blurry, the vowels clipped or jumped over – can quickly undermine your effectiveness as a public speaker. Especially if you tend to talk fast, or if you find that people often ask you to repeat yourself, consider your diction at risk.

Good diction depends on the full, supple use of the whole speaking apparatus: lips, teeth, tongue, and jaw. Improving your articulation requires repetition of the practice exercises. You can also make a start on improving your diction by being mindful of how fast you're talking, slowing down if necessary, and taking care to "finish off" each of the sounds that make up every word – especially the words at the beginning and end of each sentence.

Volume, Pitch, Pace, Cadence: Music of Speech

The human voice really is like a musical instrument or even a complete ensemble. It can run nimbly through an enormous range of notes … blare like a trumpet and purr like a cello … march briskly through a string of syllables or caress a lonely word … pound out a dirge and boogie like a ragtime tune … bring us to our feet like an anthem or put us to sleep like a lullaby. And our language gives us an infinite range of music to play.

With the mastery they have of their vocal instruments, great actors let us hear all that music, especially when they're performing the works of Shakespeare and other masters of poetic, theatrical language. But the same tricks and techniques great actors use are available to all of us; in fact, we use them every day.

Volume

It's the favorite vocal tool for many if not most speakers. After all, raising the voice or "punching up" a word or phrase with a burst of greater volume is the most natural way of getting attention or emphasizing a point.

Unfortunately, many American speakers seem to regard louder as their only vocal technique. The other end of volume control – lowering your voice, speaking softly or even in a whisper – is an enormously effective way to draw an audience toward you. The next time you're listening to a practiced public speaker, watch your fellow audience members when the speaker lowers the volume. You'll see people literally leaning forward in their seats, and you'll probably also notice them becoming quieter as well.

Pitch Variation

A term borrowed directly from music, describes a vocal dimension that we learn to use before we learn to make sentences. A toddler may not know all the words he needs or how to string them together into a request, but by raising the pitch of his voice at the end of the sound he makes, he lets us know that he's asking a question (or, more likely, asking for something he wants).

Inflection

A change in pitch applied to a single word. Inflections are very effective vocal techniques for adding meaning or force to particular words.

A downward inflection – a word that starts at one pitch and then goes down – has power and authority and also implies finality.

Use inflection to create drama.

An upward inflection – a word that starts at one pitch and then goes up at the end – can not only ask a question, like the toddler; it can also create a sense of drama, tension, and anticipation.

A series of upward inflections, the "stairway to heaven," works great when you're listing things.

A circumflexed word is one that is pitched first up, then down, or down-up, or even up-down-up. Words that have special contextual meaning or are being used to paint a picture are often circumflexed.

The rate of speech tells us a lot about urgency and importance.

Rate and Cadence

Whatever kind of music you like, part of what pleases you about it is the range of tempos and rhythms you hear, whether you're listening to a symphony, a suite, or a single song. Spoken language offers the same pleasures and the same opportunities to use pace, the speed of your talking, and cadence, the rhythmic flow of your words, to add to the interest, the meaning, and the force of what you say.

Consider, for example, a good storyteller or even just someone who tells a joke well. A good deal of his mastery lies in the way he controls and varies pace and cadence to match the various moments and movements of the story, from exposition to dramatic conflict, climax, and resolution.

In everyday life, how fast someone talks gives us a plethora of signals about what he or she is saying – its meaning, its urgency or importance, how the speaker feels about it, and more. Likewise, the cadence of speech can captivate us or bore us. Much English poetry, including the plays of Shakespeare, follows the cadence of iambic pentameter: a line of five iambs, each one made up of an unstressed syllable followed by a stressed syllable (da-DUM). For example:

When I do count the clock that tells the time ...

(the opening line of Shakespeare's Sonnet 12)

Is this the face that launched a thousand ships?

(the famous line about Helen of Troy in Marlowe's play, "Dr. Faustus")

Made weak by time and fate, but strong in will

To strive, to seek, to find, and not to yield.

(the last two lines of Tennyson's poem, "Ulysses")

The modern American playwright David Mamet has observed that iambic pentameter is actually the natural cadence of spoken English, including the highly idiomatic and often profane dialogue he writes for his own plays. In any case, it is the skillful variation in cadence that distinguishes the art of Shakespeare and other great poets and playwrights. Listening to an endless march of pure iambic pentameter, or any other regularly cadenced language, would put us to sleep if it didn't drive us crazy first.

The Pause

In speech, like in music, the strategic absence of words has special meaning, too. In my experience, the pause is the most overlooked and neglected oratorical tool among all but the most expert business and professional presenters. Silence is enormously powerful. It can bring the wandering attention of an audience back to you. It can underline the last thing you said, or build anticipation for the next thing you say. It can even get a laugh.

"Variety is the Spice of the Spoken Word."

It's a lesson every speaker must learn – and it applies to all the dimensions of vocalization. In volume, pitch, pace, and cadence, variety is your greatest ally. Keep in mind how we describe a speaker who has bored us. We say that "she droned" – meaning that her voice seemed never to vary in volume or pitch. Or, saying that "he went on and on" or spoke in a singsong way, we mimic (and ridicule) the unvaried cadence that made it seem like the speaker had no feeling for what he or she was saying – and would never finish.

Your voice is an instrument. Use it to make your presentation sing.

Mastering the music of speech is a matter of long practice. As with real music, it takes a well-trained ear in addition to a well-tuned instrument. But, just as with real music, you don't have to play everything from memory. In the theater, actors commonly mark up their scripts with various performance notes while they're rehearsing and memorizing their lines. They might underline certain words they want to emphasize or treat in some other special way … make a note about their intentions with a certain line … and use notations for passages where they want to pause, accelerate, or slow down, turn up the volume or lower it. Especially when you're going to be presenting from a verbatim script (on paper or a teleprompter), you can "score" your script in the same way.

Taking Care of Your Voice

When practicing your vocal technique, rehearsing a presentation, or just in the everyday use of your voice, it's important to take care of it. Talking is hard work, and voices get tired just like any other muscle that's used so much. When you feel your voice getting raw or raspy, when your jaws start to ache or your lungs start to feel tired, stop and be quiet, and give your vocal instrument a rest.

Actors are notorious for the variety of their voice remedies. They range from the simple, mild tea and a bit of honey and lemon, to the extreme, bags full of lozenges and supplements. If and when you're having trouble with your voice, I suggest the following steps:

Make sure you're supporting your voice with your lungs.

Think of your voice box as the light bulb and your diaphragm as the power plant.

Get some vocal rest.

Silence is a great healer. But don't think you're sparing your voice by whispering! Whispering is actually very hard on the vocal chords.

When you're losing your voice...

...take a long hot shower or place a towel over your head and breathe from a bowl of steaming hot water. Or simply breathe the steam from a cup of tea, preferably Throat Coat. Among lozenges, I've found those containing zinc are most effective.

Chill out and warm up.

The day before a big presentation, see if you can take more "quiet time" than usual to give your voice some rest; in any case, don't go to a concert or sporting event and scream your lungs out. And before going on in front of your audience, always give your voice a chance to warm up, either with a set of vocal exercises or by rehearsing a portion of your speech.

Speaking Into the Microphone

✔

Don't let the microphone make a victim of you.

Most of us have had the excruciating experience of watching and listening as a speaker fought with a microphone and lost. The tall one who hunched over and twisted his head unnaturally in an effort to make contact with the audience, because the mike was too low and he didn't take the time, or know how, to raise it. The one who manhandled the mike or chewed on it, making explosive sounds that jarred both the audience and himself. The one who stood back, intimidated by the device yet trusting it to carry her message, when all the while the mike, let alone the audience, had no chance of picking up her too-soft voice.

In short, a microphone can present you with a classic victor-versus-victim choice. Will you use it to your advantage or be defeated by it?

Microphones come in many varieties – on a stand, attached to a lectern (usually by a flexible neck), hand-held, hung around your neck or clipped to your lapel – and if public speaking is part of your professional life, you'll probably have to deal with each kind someday.

Six inches is the rule.

When using a mike on a stand or lectern, adjust it so that it's about six to ten inches from your face and below your chin. A lavaliere or clip-on mike should be placed about six inches below your chin and at or close to the center at your sternum (if it's pinned aside on one lapel, every time you turn your head the other way your voice will fade out).

Speak to the audience. Not the microphone.

In any case, remember that a microphone is designed to pick up your voice as it travels toward the audience. Speak to them, not to the mike. Talk just as you would if you didn't have a microphone, and let the technician monitoring the sound system adjust the volume to you. Just avoid hitting your consonants too hard, especially those popping p's.

Take care with your consonants.

When you combine awareness of the quality and control of your voice with active practice, you will not only change your voice – you will change your power to persuade.

Chapter 11

Physical Life: Gesture and Staging

All the World's a Stage.

In the theater, all kinds of activities take place before the show and behind the scenes to create what the audience sees and hears on the stage. The producer and her staff raise the money, buy the rights to the play, rent the theater, and hire the cast and crew … the director shapes the work of the actors, through a series of rehearsals, into a coherent and compelling enactment of the script … set, lighting, and sound designers create the onstage world where the play will take place … costume designers, makeup artists, dialogue coaches, and others ensure that each actor looks and sounds the part he or she is playing … and an army of carpenters, electricians, riggers, seamstresses, stage managers, and other technicians build the complex apparatus of the production and run it all from behind the scenes each night.

Well, guess what? When it's "Your Show, Created by You, Presented by You, Starring You," most if not all of these tasks fall on you. You are the producer, designer, and director as well as the star performer. To set yourself up for success in every presentation, you have to take responsibility for all these roles.

Think like a director to stage the room for your success.

Control Your Physical Space.

As a producer, you have to think about all the elements of the space where your show will take place, including –

- the seating and sight lines

- the acoustics and sound system

- the lighting and visuals, from programs (usually called handouts in business presentations) to PowerPoint or video

- all the elements that will affect the comfort of the audience, from the ambient temperature to refreshments and restrooms

In some venues, such as conference facilities or dedicated meeting rooms, many of these elements may be in place. You may even be familiar with them from previous events. But I caution against taking anything for granted.

Setup and Configuration

Always preview the space where you'll be presenting. Look at the setup and seating configuration. Will it serve your presentation well? Will everyone be able to see you and everything else that you want them to see (PowerPoint, product demo, video)? Can you change the setup more to your liking?

Create a dynamic physical presence.

For example, just because the chairs are in rows doesn't mean they have to be; maybe you'd prefer to have your audience seated in a semicircle so that they're aware of each other as well as of you. Just because the room has a stage at one end with a lectern and a fixed microphone doesn't mean you have to speak from there. Maybe you can arrange to use a remote microphone that will allow you to roam the stage, or the entire room, for a more dynamic physical presence during your presentation.

Save center stage for you.

When showing PowerPoint slides as part of your presentation, do not place the projection screen in the center of the stage. Instead, place the screen on your left (the audience's right) and keep center stage for yourself. That way, you will be the star while your slides play a supporting role.

Control Your Destiny: Master the Equipment.

Don't let the technology steal center stage.

When giving a presentation at an unfamiliar venue, get there ahead of time. Become familiar with the equipment you'll be using – microphones, teleprompter, overhead projector, laptop computer, and so forth – and the people you'll be relying on to operate that equipment.

Prepare a Plan B.

Think through all the technical aspects of your presentation, then make plans for a backup when things go wrong. Are your PowerPoint visuals absolutely essential to communicating what you have to say? Then you might want to bring printed copies just in case the projector goes down. Will you be delivering a verbatim speech from a teleprompter? Teleprompters have been known to fail, so carry a printed copy in your pocket.

As the producer of your presentation, be firm about the things you can control, flexible about those you can't, and wise enough to recognize the difference. You may have to make changes, even at the last minute, to what you plan to present and how it's presented. But it's better to do some last-minute scrambling than to become the victim of an awkward presentation space, unreliable equipment, or untoward events.

Directing Yourself

In the first of the presidential debates of 2004, incumbent president George W. Bush's performance earned mediocre reviews at best, even from his partisans. This was clearly on his mind when he was asked later what he had learned from the "strong women" in his life, notably his wife. "Stand up straight and don't scowl," he said. Evidently, Mrs. Bush had not minced words with him.

Body language communicates, too.

Hers was good advice for any speaker. With our reliance on language, we humans tend to forget the importance of nonverbal cues and just how much they influence what we think and feel. When you make a presentation to an audience, you speak with more than your voice. Your posture, movements, gestures, and facial expressions communicate plenty. We call it "body language" for good reason, and it can either enhance or undermine the power and even the meaning of your spoken words.

Actors are trained in the use of their bodies as well as their voices. You may be more or less aware of how you carry yourself, your posture and movements and gestures; in general, people who have trained in a sport or in any kind of dance are more "body aware." In addition, actors always have a director to tell them where to enter and exit, where to walk and stand, when to sit – even, sometimes, how to stand, how to sit, how to use their hands, and so forth. As a presenter, you can't count on having the benefit of such a resource.

So you have to direct yourself as a performer – and train yourself. To that end, here are a few basic directorial tricks and techniques I teach my clients, which you can put into practice on your own.

Find and Use Your "Money" Positions.

This is yet one more reason you should reconnoiter the venue before delivering a presentation. And take a friend or colleague with you, because you'll need someone to look at you from the audience's point of view.

Your mission: to find three "money" positions within the performance space, places to stand or sit and ways of holding yourself in each place that make you feel comfortable and help you look relaxed but authoritative. These money positions will draw your audience toward you and command their attention.

Discover positions that make you look like a million bucks.

In your "money" positions, you look and feel grounded, relaxed, and persuasive.

Seek coaching and feedback to find those positions.

As your colleague looks on, try a number of positions within the space. You may find that anchoring yourself to a physical object is comforting and helpful.

- Try leaning on the lectern, standing with your hand on a chair, writing at the white board, leaning or half-sitting on the edge of a table.

- Try holding a pen, or a clicker or a laser pointer in your hand.

- Shift your body. Feel better?

- Try putting your hand in your pocket.

Don't be surprised if the toughest position of all is simply standing in the middle of the stage or the room with nothing to hold on to – that's the scariest position for most people.

At each position, take time to adjust your posture until you feel that you "own" the space. Get feedback from your colleague. Which of your profiles, left or right, looks better? What if you shift your weight, or cross one leg in front of the other? Do you lose "presence" when you sit, or gain power? Ask your colleague, when you find a position and posture that makes you look like a million bucks, to call out, "Money!" Then keep exploring and find at least two more.

These three positions, where you know you're comfortable and look great, will serve as your home base or security zone during your presentation. You'll be able to use any or all of them as a source of confidence and comfort. Your money positions can also serve as your "itinerary": if you do nothing more than move from one to another during the course of your presentation, your performance will gain in dynamism, energy, and confident command of your audience.

The Power of Gesture

Of the many people I've watched making public presentations, most come off as lacking in energy (not to say, lifeless) because they neglect to project themselves as vital, animated human beings. They fail to exploit the power of gesture, and as a result they tend to shrink within the space around them rather than dominate it.

We know and use the power of gesture constantly and instinctively in our everyday lives. We use gestures to draw pictures in the air, to emphasize or editorialize on things we say, and to communicate how we feel about what we say. We are naturally fluent in the rich language of gesture, on both the sending and the receiving end.

Loosen up.

As the director of yourself and your presentation, you have to deal with two issues regarding your use of gesture. First, if you're the kind of person who tends to freeze up and become afraid to gesture when speaking in public, you have to learn to loosen up and reclaim the persuasive power of gesture.

Scale your gestures.

You also have to pay attention to the scale of your gesturing, and make sure it suits the space where you're presenting. It's like the difference, for actors, between acting in front of a camera or on the stage, or between acting in a theater that seats 100 and one that seats 3,000.

When you're making a presentation in a small meeting room or on video, gestures on an everyday scale will be perfectly expressive and natural. But in a medium-sized conference room or small auditorium, you have to turn up the scale and energy of your gestures. In a large auditorium or similar space, you have to make your gestures grand indeed – literally "bigger than life." This may feel unnatural at first and take some getting used to. But rest assured that, in a large space, gestures that may seem over the top to you as a presenter will read as both clear and natural to your audience.

Dare to make
the gesture fit
the space.

Staging the Presentation

In the theater it's called blocking – the movement of each actor on the stage, moment by moment – and it is meticulously devised and executed by the director and actors to clarify and enrich the meaning of the play. In a presentation, too, movement can clarify and enrich the meaning of what's being said while adding overall energy and variety. But just as in the theater, your movements must be planned and practiced.

Purposeful Movement

To start with, your movements as a presenter must be purposeful. As a coach, I've dealt with my share of frenetic presenters. Somewhere along the line these lost souls got the idea that dynamic presenting means constant movement. So they wander continuously as they talk, as if a moving target is the most compelling thing an audience has ever seen.

On the contrary, the wandering talker is both distracting and frustrating to an audience. They're so busy watching that they forget to listen, until they realize that the speaker's perpetual motion doesn't mean anything, and by then they've lost the thread.

So when you're devising your own blocking for a presentation, it's important to think about not only where you're going but why. Here are a few pointers:

Make an entrance.

Decide how you will take the stage. Having taken the stage, you will want to stay in that space for a period of time, establishing your presence with the audience. As the first chapter of your story ends, it's appropriate to move to a new part of the stage. Moving this way both signals idea change, and welcomes another part of your audience to the presentation.

Be a strolling (not wandering) storyteller.

Maybe because stories themselves have a kind of kinetic energy, movement and storytelling go well together. If your presentation includes a story or two (and I hope it does), use them to go for a stroll, but don't simply walk about aimlessly. Decide when to start moving, where you want to finish the story, and when and where – in the story and the performance space – you want to stop and anchor yourself and the audience, if only for a moment.

Move on transitions.

Virtually every speech or presentation has at least a few key transitions and pivot points. These are ideal moments to move. By changing your position, you can both signal and complement a change of subject or tone, a shift from past to present or present to future, a broadening of perspective or a raising of the stakes.

Stage in a way that punctuates your ideas.

Use the power of stillness.

Every good actor and stage director knows that a pause in the midst of movement, a sudden moment of stillness, can be as powerful as a pause in speaking. Especially when you're building to a conclusion or a call to action, you can use movement to raise the energy level; but for the moment or statement of vital importance, try standing perfectly still. Think of stillness as shining a spotlight on you and your message.

Don't Plan on "Winging It."

As both director and actor, you have complete control over and responsibility for all the details of your performance: your money positions, gestures, movements, and more. It's a lot to think about, which is why you can't afford to "wing it" when showtime rolls around. Successful presentations depend on planning and practice, which is the purpose of rehearsing.

Designing Yourself for Success

Appearance counts – and communicates. That's why, on the stage, the villain is clad in black, brides wear white, and the innocent young ingénue doesn't come onstage in a scarlet cocktail dress. As the designer of your show, you're responsible for the "look" of everything the audience sees, starting with yourself.

Does the costume suit the character?

It's not just a matter of being well groomed, but how you are groomed. Remember, you are a character in a show; what you wear is your costume, and it tells the audience something about you the moment they set eyes on you. Some leadership coaches now advise their business and professional clients to use the way they dress – say, a signature color or distinctive accessory – to establish a "personal brand." What will your costume say about your personal brand when it's showtime?

Steve Jobs could get away with the jeans-and-black-turtleneck look, even at a shareholders' meeting, but you probably cannot. Will you benefit from the strength and solidity of a tailored suit, or will an open-collar shirt and a sport coat be more appealing to your audience? If you're petite, will a "power color" like red add to your stature and authority onstage? What will you be expected to wear, and is it best to meet expectations or do you want to make a statement by pushing the envelope a bit?

Don't let "loud" clothing drown out your message.

In general, women have more choices to make about their appearance than men. I advise all my clients to avoid clothing with a complicated or "loud" design, dangling jewelry, or other distracting accessories. By distracting the eyes of your listeners, you can also distract their ears and torpedo your presentation.

Wear clothes that make you feel good.

The baseline is, your costume should be appropriate to the occasion and the venue and, ideally, flattering to your physique and your natural coloring. Above all, it should be something you feel comfortable wearing, because the more comfortable you are, the more relaxed and confident you will be as well.

Walk in your shoes.

Most actors will ask the costume shop to provide their character's shoes early in the rehearsal schedule. For the actor, this is part of a creative process of walking in the character's shoes. Many presenters wait until the actual day of the presentation to walk in their presentation shoes. Beware – if you have not rehearsed in your presentation shoes you may find yourself awkwardly clunking across the stage.

All the world's a stage. The Power of Persuasion requires that you be the master of yours.

Chapter 12

Question and Answer Techniques

Turn Question & Answer into Question & Message.

Many engagements include a question-and-answer session. Whenever this is the case, it is essential that you view the Q&A as part of your presentation. There's nothing worse than giving a great speech only to have everything go south during the Q&A because you flub a question you're not ready for, stray from your message, or lose control in the face of hostile or aggressive questioning. You must prepare for the Q&A every bit as hard as you do for the body of your presentation.

What question do you have for my message?

The point is not to try to anticipate every possible question or steel yourself to fend off the barbarians. Think positively about the Q&A: after all, it's a wonderful opportunity to drive your message home.

Every question is an opportunity.

When helping them prepare for Q&A, I like to start by reminding my clients that for every question, there are many answers. How you answer a question is your choice. In fact, you also have the right not to answer any question you don't want to answer. It is quite possible that you will decide to address (but not answer) a question and instead redirect to your message.

In any case, it's not your responsibility to answer questions the way we all did as schoolchildren – that is, in order to please the questioner. Instead, your mission is to use every question as an occasion for saying what you want to say. As you approach Q&A, turn the tables on the audience by keeping this question in mind: "What questions do you have for my message?"

Every answer reinforces your message.

You'll find that you can answer many if not most questions by repeating something you've already said in your presentation – taking the opportunity to repeat a key message. When a question requires you to give more information about a topic you addressed in your presentation, go ahead – but be careful not to overelaborate or wander off on a tangent. Instead, quickly transition from the "new" information to the message it clarifies or supports.

Keep your message mantra front and center in your awareness during Q&A, and reinforce it at every opportunity.

Prepare your own questions.

And what if no one is ready to ask a question or if you don't get the questions you want? Make sure you have your own questions at the ready, such as –

"You may be wondering …" or

"One question I'm often asked is …"

Chances are, this will prime the pump and the audience will soon join in the dialogue.

This is your
Q & A
Playbook.
Use it!

Friendly, Challenging and Hostile Questions

There are many techniques for handling Q&A not just successfully but gracefully. We'll begin with baseline tips and then proceed to ways of handling difficult and hostile questions.

Tone and Attitude

You need the same tone and attitude during Q&A as during a presentation: confident, passionate, informative, and interactive. Q&A is a time for you to shine; take advantage of it. Remember, you are the expert.

You are also building relationships; Q&A is a great time to come out from behind the podium or table, move toward your audience, and engage them as a group and as individuals. Use people's names if you know them. Start each answer by responding directly to the questioner, but as you transition to a more general point (ideally, one of your key messages from the body of the presentation), take in the whole audience.

Active Listening

Remember that your listening will be judged as much as your answers. Listen to the questioner, not just the question, with an open body posture, good eye contact, and a display of genuine interest.

Listen carefully. Take time to hear the question and make sure you understand it before responding. Ask the questioner to clarify if necessary. A tried-and-true technique for starting an answer is to repeat the question. In larger venues where the audience may not be able to hear every question from the floor, you may have to repeat the question so that everyone will understand your answer.

"Gosh, I Like You!"

While you're listening to and answering questions, think about how much you like the audience or the person asking the questions. Thinking "Gosh, I like you!" will give you sparkle, and may even inspire you to smile. This simple technique is especially useful in on-camera interviews, because what you're thinking and feeling is easy to read in your face close-up. It will also give you the extra energy you need in the two-dimensional realm of video.

Start With the Conclusion.

During Q&A, people don't have the time or the patience to wait for you to build to a conclusion. Answer with your Powerbite!

Stay Within Your Area of Expertise!

If you don't know the answer, say so. Never try to answer a question when you don't know the answer. During friendly Q&A it's perfectly okay to say, "Good question – I really don't have an answer. But …" – and then you can promise the questioner to find the answer later, and/or transition the dialogue to a topic that is "solid ground" for you.

Listen for Categories of Questions.

As you become more comfortable with Q&A, you will become adept at categorizing questions presented to you. This way, you can take advantage of pre-crafted answers and Powerbites to answer types of questions.

For instance, when preparing a team for a high stakes presentation, we were able to build responses to several likely question categories:

- *Why change* questions – tell an aspirational story or cautionary tale.

- *Price* questions – answer with value Powerbite.

- *Implementation* questions – answer with winning process Powerbite.

- The *hand-holding* questions – sell our experienced team.

- The *fear of failure* questions – celebrate our track record of successes.

Every question is an opportunity to reiterate your message.

More Difficult Q & A

When questions get more challenging, they require the mastery of additional techniques.

Say it and Stop.

Especially during potentially difficult Q&A, briefly give your best answer and stop. Project confidence that you have successfully answered the question and need to say nothing more. Keep in mind as well that professional interviewers – including lawyers taking depositions, news reporters, and financial analysts – are practiced in using silence to intimidate and draw people into saying more than they need or want to. Don't give in. Remember, the more words you use, the more rope you will extend to hang yourself.

Touch, Bridge, and Go.

While "Say it and Stop" will put the ball back in the court of your questioner, "Touch, Bridge and Go" helps you drive more aggressively to your message.

Think of the "touch" as a way of acknowledging the question without going deep into an answer. Think of the "bridge" as the language connecting to the message you wish to deliver. Having built the bridge, "Go" to the message.

Answer the question they should have asked.

Touch, Bridge and Go in action:

(Touch) "I understand how you might focus on this one example, (Bridge) but the real story here is …(Go) "

(Touch) "That's a great question and we'll have to sort out those details, (Bridge) But there's a bigger issue here …(Go)"

(Touch) "Glad you brought that up. I'm happy to send you details on how we'll tackle that … (Bridge) More important to the success of this project is …(Go)"

(Touch) "I hear your concern about resourcing the teams – who wouldn't love a bigger budget …" (Bridge) but my main point here has to do with the implementation of a better workflow … (Go) let me go deeper into the new …"

Define, Don't Defend.

Questioners sometimes want to focus on the "negatives" – past mistakes or failures, opportunities missed, uncertainties, and so forth. Don't be defensive, and don't be drawn into dissecting the past. When you start talking about why something's broken, it's easy to start assigning blame.

Instead, focus on what has been learned or what you're doing to overcome the challenges or improve the process. Define the promise of the future rather than defending against the disappointments of the past.

If You Don't Have the Answer, Sell the Process.

Often you simply won't have good answers to tough questions. You will lack the metrics, you won't have the program in place, or you will be in the early days of building out the solution. In cases like these you will be best served to "sell the process."

When you share details of a process that has rationality and has integrity, you gain credibility while diffusing the urgent need to know.

Buy Time.

You can't anticipate every question; audience members come up with the darndest things. There will be times when you're surprised or caught off guard by a question or comment from the audience. Don't panic or hurry your answer – you may live to regret it. Instead, buy time to think about your answer.

"Taking time to think" is authentic and authoritative.

There are three ways to buy time:

Ask the person to repeat the question.

Rephrase the question in a way you wish to answer it.

This goes to a useful rule of thumb for all Q&A: "Don't answer the question they asked; answer the question they should have asked."

Take time to consider your answer before speaking.

Though least used, the third technique is actually the most powerful. Taking your time, being deliberate, gives you an air of authority. It also adds to your credibility, because the audience sees that you're actually thinking about the question and not just spewing out some prepackaged pablum.

Don't Break into Jail.

Avoid bringing up new issues or perspectives that might intrigue the audience and take them off your message. Use good judgment by staying away from topics that send you down a rat hole because they:

- are too complicated

- introduce an alternative point of view

- are fraught with controversy

Never Repeat Poison Words.

When they say "train wreck!" your job is to think of the antonym ("smooth sailing"). Use your imagery instead of theirs. "That's not how I would characterize it … the way we see it is …"

Move the
problem away
from you.

Punt.

For more challenging or hostile Q&A, become expert at punting.

Be ready with the language and style of punting. Smile and stay engaged and confident while you punt. Always follow your "no" with a transition to something you prefer to discuss.

Examples of punting:

- "That's a technical question that falls outside my area of expertise; let me put you in touch with …"

- "The development team is probably your best source for an answer to that question; let's connect you with them …"

- "I have expertise in the disciplinary aspect of your question but for the complete answer we'd want to bring in an expert on employment agreements; let me address the disciplinary question …"

Questions You Don't Have to Answer

People sometimes ask inappropriate questions – questions that you simply won't have to answer. They may try to blindside you with new "information" or a "phantom" authority. For example, "According to the recent article in …" Or they may ask questions in such a way as to trick you, trap you, or box you in; for example, "Isn't it true that …?"

You don't have to answer these "gotcha" questions. The artistry is in turning them into opportunities. In general, all you have to do is transition from your refusal to address their question (with or without giving your reason) to something you do want to talk about. Here are several examples:

Q: Seeks proprietary information.

A: "That's proprietary information that I can't share with you, but what I can tell you is …"

Q: Asks for a legal opinion or information.

A: "That's a legal issue and I'm not a lawyer. But I can say …"

Q: Probes for information about a specific employee.

A: "We don't speak publicly about personnel issues. What I can tell you is …"

Q: Probes for information about a particular individual.

A: "Out of respect for Mr. Smith's privacy, I'm afraid I can't address that. Perhaps he would be willing to discuss it with you. In the meantime, what I want to emphasize is …"

Q: "What if…?"

A: "I wouldn't want to speculate."

Q: "When will you stop strong-arming Alpha Corporation…?"

A: "We have a very good relationship with Alpha Corporation, and …" or "We think competition is good for our industry and our customers …"

Q: "What three mistakes…?

A: "What we should be talking about are our three greatest successes …"

Q: "How would X respond?"

A: "You'll have to ask X."

Q: "What is the worst…?"

A: "That would be speculating. Let's focus on the real issue here …"

✔

Do not answer "gotcha" questions.

Q: "It was recently stated that..." or "An article in last week's news said..."

A: "I haven't heard that ..." or "I haven't seen that article."

Q: "... yes or no?" or "Is that true?"

A: "In fact, that's not a yes or no question ..." or "I don't think it's as simple as that. When we look at all the facts ..."

When Challenging Morphs to Hostile

Q & A is inherently challenging. But sometimes it gets downright hostile. You never know when and where a "poison pill" or "pot-stirrer" will appear. Always anticipate hostile questions, no matter what the topic or the venue.

When you sense hostility in a question or questioner, first remind yourself to maintain your key communication techniques: an open and relaxed posture, a resonant and varied voice, concise and clear answers.

Consider your options.

Again, you don't have to answer any question, especially one that's off-topic, clearly intended to set you up to make a mistake, put you on the defensive, or lead to another hostile question.

Empathy Without Culpability

Several tools can help you through tough situations.

In business and professional life, just as everywhere else, bad things happen, mistakes get made, people are disappointed or hurt. If you're conducting a Q&A in the wake of such difficulties, you may have to deal with the tough questions that result. In these circumstances, questioners often express anger or frustration. The best way to deal with such moments is an approach I call empathy without culpability.

First, you acknowledge the feeling that's being expressed:

"I see this is really upsetting to you." Take the time to let them know they've been heard. Sometimes they just need to know someone is listening.

Then you empathize:

"I am deeply saddened by your experience ... " or " I think everyone here can relate to your frustration." Be empathetic without accepting the blame.

Finally, bridge from the negative to the positive:

"Our big concern now is moving forward and building a better …" This often means moving from the past to the future.

Through empathy without culpability, you validate the feelings of those asking tough questions without agreeing to take the blame.

Avoid a One-on-One Dialogue.

Never allow Q&A to become a dialogue between you and just one questioner. Don't let a questioner with an agenda follow up with a second question. Instead, take control by transitioning to another section of the audience: "So as you can see, we're working hard to tackle that challenge … (turning your body away from the questioner) "… now I think I saw that you had a question over here. How can I help you?"

Triangulate.

At a certain moment in Q&A you may feel that the boundary between the problem and you is disappearing. The hostility and level of accusation is high as is the frustration. One last option, which is highly preferable to the phrase "let's take that off line," is to triangulate.

Triangulation is simple. Separate yourself from the problem. Write the problem on a white board or flip chart or use language to place the problem somewhere other than in your hands.

By separating yourself from the problem, then turning to face the problem alongside the questioner, you change the nature of the engagement. "And so I think I've put the question up on the board as you described it. Let's take a look together and see how we can solve it."

Triangulation creates a space between you and the tough issue.

Facing the Media

As a media trainer for high stakes interviews, product launches and earnings calls, I implore you: Do not enter the unfair world of the media without engaging in dedicated preparation and coaching!

That said, the lines are blurring between what we think of as privileged, confidential communication and what ends up as broad distribution of your latest quotable quote. Our public presentations and panel discussions are the subject of instant digital distribution. We live in the world of tiny microphones, video cameras, Tweets, YouTube and blogs. Don't be surprised if you learn that your presentation or communication is being instantly distributed. The general public has become a form of the "press."

Stay on Message.

When facing questions in these scenarios, you will be best served by staying zealously on message. First apply a heavy dose of the previously mentioned strategy. Don't answer the question they ask, answer the question they should have asked. Stated another way: What questions do you have for my Powerbite? Speak from the Powerbite by hitting the conclusion, the evidence and the "so what" to the point of redundancy. Use all the techniques referenced in the challenging and hostile question section. Then add the following strategies and tactics to the mix:

Tweets, YouTube and blogs are powerful media of the general public.

Understand the New Ground Rules.

Dealing with professional (and non-professional) journalists is a form of Q&A with its own special challenges. It is not a conversation. That means you cannot build on ideas and hope to have your statements received in context. As a rule of thumb, try to make sure that anything you say would be complete and coherent if appearing as a tweet.

Be the Editor.

They cannot print what you do not say.

When you choose to speak, know how much space your interviewer is likely to use for your message or quotable quote. (For example: national broadcast media averages 6 seconds per soundbite.) Edit your words to fit the medium. If your soundbite is too long, you will become the victim of their edit. You'll scream that you were misquoted or taken out of context … but it will be your own fault.

Correct False Assumptions/Statements.

When an interviewer states a false assumption, stop him or her and establish the real facts before going on.

Never Lie.

Reporters don't like to be lied to any more than anyone else – except perhaps the ones who know they can make their reputation by catching you out on a lie.

No Jargon or Acronyms

Your business or profession, like most these days, is probably rife with jargon, acronyms, and assorted "insider" language. If you want to be quoted in the press, speak in plain language that the general reader will understand.

Never Get Drawn into a Fight.

Mark Twain suggested one should "never fight with people who buy ink by the barrel." Argue with a reporter or interviewer and you will lose – it's as simple as that.

Basic survival
tips for
all media
transactions

No Sarcasm

More than one career has been ruined by a snide remark or poisonous quip that took on a life of its own in the media.

Be Careful About Jokes.

Humor doesn't always "play" in print or even on video. Besides, humor can be double-edged. What's funny to you may be confusing or even insulting to someone else. Before using humor in front of the press (or any audience, for that matter), pre-test it with a trusted colleague.

Lessons from Broadcast Media Training

Recently I've been helping print reporters expand beyond the written word to the world of broadcast media. These folks know that the more media they master, the more impact they will have. But becoming broadcast savvy is not a simple challenge. The reporter must take the best of the written word and reshape it for the short form of television. The rules are different, the cadence more rapid, and the conversational back and forth unfamiliar. And then there is the issue of style. How you look and sound is as important as what you actually say. In the age of CNBC and You Tube, we could all use a little broadcast media savvy. Here are a few of the tips to consider.

Be TV Savvy.

The more that you understand television production the better you will be. Attune yourself to roles and process – the Executive Producer, Senior Producer, Technical Director, Show Producer; the "soup to nuts" of a single interview. The victor will know who is who and be familiar with the process and rhythm of show production. The victor will engage the producer early in the process, ask questions and suggest provocative questions or compelling visuals.

Sit Up Straight.

Stylistically, sit up straight – lead from the heart – animate to counteract the flatness of the 2D medium. Use all the gestures you would at a fun party. Use compelling language but keep it short and sharp and give air so the follow-up question can be asked. Insist on hair and make-up assistance.

Know your Process.

Determine what you need to do to make success inevitable, from the moment you are contacted right up until the moment of the show. If you don't have the gift of gab you may need to practice your spoken word messages multiple times before sitting down in front of the camera. If you do have the gift of gab you may need to spend most of your time prioritizing and refining to make sure you say what you need to say in fewer words.

Answer the question they should have asked.

Focus on the Key Message.

From a messaging point of view I recommend you reduce the sauce by focusing on the key message of your story. What's the lead, the key message, the headline, the takeaway? And equally important "So what?" why should your audience care? What does it mean to the market, the consumer, or the investor? Don't answer the question they ask, answer the question they should have asked – and the one you are prepared to answer.

Take advantage of "Just in Time" preparation.

The victim will sit passively while being hooked up to microphone and get more nervous as each moment passes. The victor will engage the producer and or interviewer and attempt to impact the content and quality of the interview. Try to discuss with the interviewer the key points, flow and take-away message of your upcoming interview. Point out the dead ends or questions that fall outside your expertise. Develop a relationship before the red light goes on.

Talk to the Viewers.

On many occasions it will be perfectly reasonable for you to go beyond strictly answering the interviewer's questions. Broaden your answer and speak to the viewing audience. – "For those out there considering … My message to people out there is …"

Give them at least one "Gosh Moment."

Viewers should watch you and say to themselves "Gosh – I didn't know that … or … Gosh, I hadn't been tracking that … or … Gosh, I've never thought of it that way before."

This is, of course, just a beginning. If you do have a high-stakes opportunity, you will be well served to do as the Super Bowl Champs do – get great coaching – and practice, practice, practice before the big event.

With these strategies and tools in hand, you are ready to turn question and answer scenarios into question and message successes.

Exercise: Turn Q & A into Q & M

A "key message powerbite" gives you a head start on answers that reiterate your point.

What Questions Do They Have for Your Message?

A Q & A session is an opportunity to reiterate your key message as often as possible.

Define Your Key Messages.

Craft your key message for an upcoming high-stakes persuasion.

If you use the Powerbite to build your message, you'll find you can re-use the conclusion, three pieces of supporting evidence and the "so what?" as answers, driving your point deeper with each question.

Conclusion

Evidence

Evidence

Evidence

So What? (Meaning)

Answer the Questions They Should Have Asked.

Now, anticipate three tough questions and draft a response using the content from your key message Powerbite. Or, build a response using "touch, bridge and go": acknowledge the question, insert a bridge and go to your key message.

It's Showtime!

It's Showtime!

There's no business like show business
Like no business I know
Everything about it is appealing
Everything the traffic will allow
Nowhere can you have that happy feeling
When you are stealing that extra bow
— From Irving Berlin's "Annie Get Your Gun"

Just as in the theater, *you* will have an opening night; your reputation on the line, the critics judging you … in print, on blogs, at the office, on the street.

I have good news. Having applied the power of persuasion to your "show," you have done everything you can to guarantee success. You will bring your professional passion to the stage. You've listened and played detective, so you know your audience and the obstacles to success. By bringing insight to your presentation, you have raised the bar and made your offer more compelling.

But that's not all. You have taken the fire hose of information and given your audience a gift by reducing it to make it crisp and memorable. Expert as you are in the delivery vehicles, you have made intelligent choices as to when to use the Powerbite, the story or perhaps even the slow build to a conclusion. Thanks to the preparation protocol, your presentation has attended to the who, where, when and why. You have a clear objective.

The structure of your presentation is artful; easy for you to navigate and easy for the audience to follow, understand and remember. Through rehearsal you have made the difficult easy, the easy habitual and you are poised to make the habitual artful. Choices have been made about staging and gesture, pacing and tone. You're confident because you know how to manage the questions that may come during or after your presentation.

And so … what is to be done?

The clock is ticking; the audience is settling in. As it should be, your heart is fluttering – wouldn't it be too bad if you didn't care enough to feel a bit of the pre-show excitement?

Your show will be a smashing success.

In the theater, the director will often share final words of advice with the cast.

"Let the audience response tell you where to go."

"Listen."

"You've done all you can, now just tell the story."

"Take a breath."

In sports, the coach often makes the pre-game speech.

"Win one for the Gipper."

"This is the moment when all your hard work pays off."

"Have faith in yourself and your team."

When making a presentation, there may be no director or coach to bring you home.. What should you say to yourself?

You may be tempted to go back and attend to the building blocks of your persuasion or review your technique. You might find yourself checking the notes, thinking about your opening sentence, trying to run through a story that will be pivotal to the presentation, thinking about a vocal inflection. I wouldn't blame you for having this impulse; after all, the work you have done represents strings in a parachute that might promote a soft landing.

Ahh, but there is the rub. If you look back, you might just turn to stone. You'll be focusing on landing instead of flying. You'll be focused on the past and not the future. You'll be focused on technique and not performance. Music, theater and dance audiences have no interest in performers who show off technique. The same applies in presenting. Audiences know something is amiss when a presenter watches herself and her technique while presenting.

But I've not answered the question. What is to be done?

At the beginning of many of my workshops, I play a simple game with the group. We toss an imaginary ball from person to person while saying their name. As the game progresses and as we add more balls to the circle, a lesson emerges. To be successful you have to connect! On the most basic level, you must make sure the person with whom you are communicating gets the ball. You cannot achieve this by playing catch *at* them. You can only achieve it by playing catch *with* them.

It's time to fly!

I believe if you commit to connecting, *right here, right now, in the moment* with your audience; if you dare to be present and to have faith in all of the preparation that came before, the strings of the parachute will be cut, the communication will have begun, and you, the fully evolved, persuasive presenter will soar.

You have mastered the Power of Persuasion – It's Showtime! and it's time to fly.

Appendix 1

Top 10 Ways to Handle Nerves

1. Practice and rehearse your material – more than you think you need to. This includes talking through and visualizing the story arc of your communication.

2. Be clear on your objectives – what do you want from the audience? Remember, it's about them, not you.

3. Arrive early to set up the room and test the equipment.

4. Having arrived early, greet the audience as they arrive. Engage, interview and make connections. When you begin speaking, use those people you've talked to as safe harbors in the audience.

5. Find your "money" positions and get into one before speaking.

6. Breathe. A good physical warm up, workout or long walk the morning of a high stakes presentation will help. Take a deep breath right before you begin.

7. Start with a story. Stories are easy to tell and give you access to your best, most relaxed communication style.

8. Within the first two minutes, shift the focus from you to the audience. Ask them to take a moment to reflect or engage another audience member in considering a topic or answering a question.

9. Carry and refer to your notes. Give yourself permission to look at them.

10. If you are having to sit and wait because you are one of many presentations, actively engage in the presentation prior to yours by taking notes rather than ruminating on your presentation. This will allow you to be more present and keep you from working yourself into a tizzy.

The number one way to calm your nerves: practice!

Appendix 2

Presentation Effectiveness

Feedback Guide

This guide covers the key characteristics of an effective presentation. Ask your friends and colleagues to use it to provide feedback about your presentations during rehearsal and/or performance.

You may also wish to use it yourself to make notes about speeches and presentations that you attend as an audience member, as a way of developing your eye and ear for what makes a presentation effective and persuasive.

Ask your co-workers to use this guide to help assess the effectiveness of your persuasion

Speaker:

Presentation title or topic:

Date:

Compelling

Does the speaker capture and command the attention of the audience? How?

Strong Objective

Does the speaker seem to have a clear objective? What is it?

On Task

Does the speaker stay on course and repeat the key messages?

Use of Physical Space

Does the speaker use the performance space effectively, moving and positioning himself or herself to provide variety and enhance meaning?

Use of Visuals

How does the speaker use visuals to enhance the presentation? Are they effective? Does the speaker interact with the visuals in an effective manner?

Gestures

Does the speaker use physical life and gestures effectively to enhance delivery? How?

✔

Or use this guide to help you learn from other speakers.

Connection

Does the speaker connect with the audience, through good eye contact and/or by other means?

Relaxation

Does the speaker seem relaxed?

Language

How does the speaker use language clearly and forcefully? What phrases or choices of words are most effective? What choices, such as excessive jargon or unexplained acronyms, create confusion or otherwise detract from the presentation?

Voice

Does the speaker project his or her voice well, and in a pleasing tone? Does the speaker use any of the following vocal techniques effectively?

- Volume variations

- Pitch variations

- Inflection variations

- Rate/cadence variations, including dramatic pauses

Owning the Talk

Does the speaker personalize the presentation and make it his or her own, or does it seem like a "canned" talk?

The Whole Package

Is the speaker's combined physical, vocal, and intellectual energy sufficient to engage and move the audience?